PRAISE FOR *OBSESSED*

"A lucid and engaging playbook on why 'brand' is the most fundamental, human, and engaging element of any great venture—why it's the business DNA, and not just the representation of it. *Obsessed* keeps you anchored to the raison d'etre!"

—David Bell, cofounder and president, Idea Farm Ventures

"We're all prey to our obsessions. (Yes, even you). Ready to find out why? This book will show you."

—Sally Hogshead. *New York Times* bestselling author of *How the World Sees You* and *Fascinate*

"Clear, useful, and refreshingly honest, this is a practical manual on how modern marketing actually works. Buy a copy for everyone on your team."

—Seth Godin, author of *This Is Marketing*

"I look to invest in campanies with promising new models and a focus on brand that starts with a true understanding of the consumer. Emily Heyward's book is a fascinating look into how branding really works and why it matters."

—Kirsten Green, founding partner, Forerunner Ventures

"When we started Casper, our brand strategy affected every decision—and in this book, Emily Heyward shows you how. Anyone starting a company should read this."

—Philip Krim, cofounder and CEO of Casper

"The startup landscape is always shifting, but across every category we're looking to invest in people who understand the power of brand. This book, with Emily's valuable advice, is essential for getting it right."

—Ben Lerer, managing partner at Lerer Hippeau and CEO of Group Nine Media

"*Obsessed* is a clear, informed blueprint founders and marketers can use to craft a resilient brand—one that will not only break new ground, but inspire an unforgettable customer connection."

—Nir Eyal, bestselling author of *Hooked* and *Indistractable*

"Nobody understands the development of modern brands better than Emily Heyward. In *Obsessed*, Heyward illuminates the DNA of brands that move us and enhance our daily lives. By surgically deconstructing the art of branding and the lessons we must learn, Heyward outfits us to be brand builders and stewards that transform products and industries."

—Scott Belsky, founder of Behance and author of *The Messy Middle*

OBSESSED

OBSESSED

Building a Brand People
Love from Day One

EMILY HEYWARD

PORTFOLIO / PENGUIN

PORTFOLIO / PENGUIN
An imprint of Penguin Random House LLC
penguinrandomhouse.com

Most Portfolio books are available at a discount when purchased in quantity for
sales promotions or corporate use. Special editions, which include personalized covers,
excerpts, and corporate imprints, can be created when purchased in large quantities.
For more information, please call (212) 572-2232 or e-mail specialmarkets@
penguinrandomhouse.com. Your local bookstore can also assist with discounted
bulk purchases using the Penguin Random House corporate Business-to-Business
program. For assistance in locating a participating retailer, e-mail
B2B@penguinrandomhouse.com.

LIBRARY OF CONGRESS CATALOGING-IN-PUBLICATION DATA
Names: Heyward, Emily (Chief brand officer), author.
Title: Obsessed : building a brand people love from day one / Emily Heyward.
Description: New York : Portfolio / Penguin, [2020] | Includes index.
Identifiers: LCCN 2019059648 (print) | LCCN 2019059649 (ebook) |
ISBN 9780593084311 (hardcover) | ISBN 9780593084328 (ebook)
Subjects: LCSH: Branding (Marketing) | Creative ability
in business. | Success in business.
Classification: LCC HF5415.1255 .H49 2020 (print) | LCC HF5415.1255 (ebook) |
DDC 658.8/27—dc23
LC record available at https://lccn.loc.gov/2019059648
LC ebook record available at https://lccn.loc.gov/2019059649

Printed in the United States of America
4th Printing

Book design by Lauren Kolm and Meighan Cavanaugh

For Michelle
Best friends forever, baby

CONTENTS

Author's Note   ix

Introduction   xi

1. Fear of Death   1

2. Elevate to the Emotional   25

3. Sense of Self   49

4. Creating Connection   75

5. Strength in Focus   99

6. Redefine Expectations   125

7. Embrace Tension   149

8. Make it Personal   173

   Conclusion   199

   Acknowledgments   203

   Index   209

AUTHOR'S NOTE

THROUGHOUT THE BOOK, I'VE INDICATED THE COMPANIES with whom I've worked closely as clients of Red Antler. The other examples are drawn from my observations as a brand builder and consumer, but I have no direct relationship to them. In both cases, the book is filled with companies whose stories are still being written. Some will inevitably experience failure, and some may experience scandal (a few already have). In the course of writing the book, I had to go back and edit chapters as a founder came under fire or a boycott erupted, but I'm not going to be able to pull the book off shelves and scribble in future updates. Such is the risk of writing a book about modern brands in real time. I've chosen companies that I admire because they represent universal principles of brand building, but brands are run by people, and people continue to be imperfect, even within the idealistic promises of today's startup culture. All of this is to say that I am not endorsing any bad behavior, past, present, or future, by the teams that I've included. But please, founders, just be good, okay?

INTRODUCTION

YOU DON'T NEED TO WORK IN VENTURE CAPITAL OR GRAD-
uate from Stanford business school to recognize that we're in the
midst of a consumer startup revolution. Scroll through your Instagram feed, and you're more likely to see a beautiful, compelling ad
from a brand you've never heard of than you are to see an old favorite. The barriers to entry for launching a business get lower every
day, which means new brands are popping up at a whack-a-mole
velocity. The old gatekeepers no longer exist; you don't need to be
able to afford a TV ad or get a place on the shelf at a major retail
chain in order to get in front of people. Every category is up for grabs,
and traditional leading brands are seeing their businesses slowly erode
as hundreds of small companies encroach on their territory. As category after category gets disrupted, as competition gets fiercer, it's no

longer enough to have a great idea, or a better price, or faster shipping. Founders need to be thinking about brand from *before* day one; it needs to be embedded in their culture from the very start. They need to build a brand that people will fall madly in love with at first sight, and they need to do it before they even launch.

It wasn't always this way. When I graduated from college in 2001, I took a job at a large global advertising agency to work on huge, established brands, many of which had been around for literally a century. Our role at the agency was to create new TV campaigns every year that would generate renewed excitement and energy for old, familiar things. I learned a ton about how the world's oldest and largest consumer goods companies approach brand building, and the rigor that goes into defining a target audience, sharpening a consumer insight, developing a clear and succinct brand strategy, and then using that strategy to guide all communications. I loved my job, and I met some of the smartest and most creative people I've ever known.

But after a few years, I grew frustrated. TV advertising was becoming less and less dominant, and we were tasked with coming up with new messages about brands that simply didn't feel relevant, with no power to affect the brands or products themselves. I started to describe my job as "what new thing can we say about yogurt this year?" (The answer: not much.) I felt that we were solving the wrong problems.

I was looking for a change, and my friend JB, eventually my cofounder, brought me on to help him run the New York office for a New Zealand–based creative agency. It was 2006 and the startup scene in New York was just gaining steam. Because we were small, we started meeting entrepreneurs, people who had amazing ideas for businesses that could fundamentally transform behaviors—people who were using innovation to solve real problems.

They didn't need advertising, at least not yet, but we discovered in our conversations that they knew very little about how to build a brand, or even what that really meant. We saw an opportunity to take everything we had learned working with large global brands and apply it to launching and growing new businesses that we wanted to see in the world.

Our belief was that brand is an engine that drives business growth, and the sooner businesses incorporate brand thinking, the more set up for success they'll be. We struck out on our own and founded Red Antler in 2007 to test that hypothesis by partnering with founders to help them embed this perspective from day one.

Years later, Red Antler has grown to over a hundred people, but we still mostly work with startups. We've played a key role in launching some of the most successful and exciting new brands in the world, helping create billions of dollars of value. In fact, half of our clients are "pre-launch," which means that we meet founding teams before they've launched their businesses, and help them to create the entire consumer-facing experience through the lens of brand.

When we first started Red Antler, many people questioned whether founders should invest in brand before they've proven product-market fit and started to gain traction. But our philosophy is "brand early, not often." This directly contradicts the "lean startup," "test to success" approaches that many earlier tech companies embraced. Today, it feels like a new company launches every second, and you can no longer get an idea out there, see if it has momentum, and then iterate on your brand as you would on a set of software features. If you're launching a particular business, you can be sure that someone else is too. This phenomenon plays out in Hollywood, where you end up with two almost identically themed movies coming out in the same year. (Or with kids' names—you think you're so creative, and then there are four Marlows on the playground.)

The same cultural forces and gaps in the market that lead one founder to launch a direct-to-consumer contact lens business are leading someone else to do the same. And the time frame for a trend to demonstrate itself has only gotten more intense—it used to be that over the course of a year, we would notice that more and more people were launching businesses in a certain category. Now, within a month, we'll sometimes meet with three different teams launching nearly identical ideas. Because it's so much easier to get things off the ground, and because technology has lowered the barriers to entry for everyone, the difference in success largely boils down to brand.

Q: Okay. So what is a brand?

Don't confuse the importance of brand with what you might traditionally think of as "branding": a name, a logo, fonts, colors, a tagline. Those elements matter a great deal, but they're a piece of the puzzle, the outward expression of what a brand is all about. There's the part that people can see (important), and then there's the part they feel (more important!). Leading brands are able to form deep emotional connections because they stand for something that people care about. When I talk about brand, what I'm actually talking about is what a business stands for, at its very core. In order to drive success in today's consumer landscape, brand cannot just be a layer that sits on top; it has to be baked into the business itself. Many founders think that "branding" is something to worry about once they've figured out the important stuff, a box to check at the end of the process. But that couldn't be further from the truth. Brand should be the ongoing, guiding force that drives how a business behaves. Whether you're a startup founder, an aspiring entrepreneur, or a brand marketer, there's a lot to be learned from the companies who get it right in the early days. These are the ones who come out swinging, and it isn't long before people have a hard time remembering the world without them. These companies so fundamentally transform a category that they become the benchmark for others looking to do the same ("I want to be the Warby Parker of shower caps/dog food/laundry detergent"). These category-defining brands may look like overnight successes, but the work began long before consumers were even aware these companies existed. I can't tell you how many times entrepreneurs will point to a past success and try to explain how their business is actually much harder, much more of a challenge than, say, Casper, the mattress business we helped launch. And I'll have to explain to them that before Casper was Casper, no one thought it was possible to sell mattresses online—many investors laughed at the idea. It was only after we built a brand with which people fell madly in love that Casper's success felt obvious, a foregone conclusion. It looks easy because the connections these businesses build with their consumers feel so natural, so human, like a lifelong friend that you've somehow only just met.

In this book, I will outline the core principles that define the new generation of brand leaders, brands like Casper, Sweetgreen, Allbirds, Warby Parker, and Glossier. As I'll indicate throughout the book, some of these brands are my clients, companies that we've partnered closely with to create brand-led experiences. Others are companies that I admire, through my perspective as both a brand builder and a consumer. By examining the new rules of brand, I will demonstrate not only what it takes to create a category-defining business but also how this new generation is changing the game for everyone.

In chapter 1, I'll look at what it means to ground everything you do in the problem you're solving for people and the deepest, truest needs of your consumers, ensuring that what you're building is relevant.

In chapter 2, I'll talk about the importance of moving beyond the functional, building a brand that is rooted in a deep emotional benefit. We'll examine why the emotional resonance of a brand can't just be a nice, pretty story you tell but instead needs to connect to the value that your business actually brings to people's lives.

In chapter 3, I'll look at how today's successful brands tap into their consumers' sense of self and identity, aligning their values with the people they're trying to reach.

Chapter 4 is about community, and the strength of brands that create a sense of connection across their audience.

In chapter 5, I'll talk about the importance of focus, and how the most successful brands of today aren't afraid to put a stake in the ground about who they're for and what they stand for.

Chapter 6 is about breaking convention and redefining consumer expectations. We'll look at how brands have rewritten the rules to build connections in categories where no one even thought brand mattered.

In chapter 7, I'll dispel the old myth about the importance of consistency, and look at how tension and surprise play a critical role in today's brand playbook.

Lastly, chapter 8 examines the role of the founder, and the power of revealing the human side of a business in order to drive brand love.

Throughout the book, I'll look at examples that embody what it means to build a brand that people love from day one, from huge successes like Airbnb, Everlane, and Sweetgreen, to growing startups whose stories are still being written. These are businesses that understand that every single consumer interaction—from talking with customer service, to shopping on a website, to reading an interview with the founder—counts as "brand." Throughout the customer journey, standout brands balance newness and surprise with a feeling of deep, intimate connection. It never seems like they're trying to sell you something, or convince you of something; instead, it feels that you're in a relationship based on a shared set of values.

These are the brands that people obsess over. Consumers become obsessed when they feel a personal connection to a brand that goes beyond the product itself. Customers follow these brands on social media, eagerly awaiting their next offering. A word that used to imply a troubling, perhaps dangerous level of preoccupation has now become part of the consumer and editorial vernacular: "I'm *obsessed* with my new [jeans, candle, AirPods, meditation app]." "Meet our latest obsession." There are over ten million posts on Instagram that use #obsessed, and in addition to puppy photos (duh), they include pictures of mugs, jewelry, couches, makeup, sneakers, you name it. And people are not just gushing about these brands to their friends and enthusiastically posting about them; they incorporate the products into their own identities. Ultimately, their alignment with these brands says something about themselves.

Of course, the catch is that if you're going to build a brand that is rooted in principles, those principles need to be upheld. It's totally possible that by the time you're reading this, one or more of these businesses will have been called out for some shady practice or offensive tweet or immoral investor, something that flies in the face of what they purport to stand for. Consumers have begun to hold businesses accountable for their behavior, which is more evidence of the new set of expectations that companies need to meet through and through. People aren't making choices based on what their parents always bought—they're seeking out companies that align with their core beliefs and to which they can relate on a human level. That's why brand today is so much more than an aesthetic layer, and why it plays such a key role in a startup's trajectory. Brand needs to be ingrained in a business's very reason for being, which is why it's so important to get it right from the beginning.

Q: *Are you going to tell us the secret to creating the next great hit?*

That's why we're here! Keep reading, and you'll find deep firsthand knowledge of what goes on behind the scenes of successful startups, pre- and post-launch. You'll learn about how consumer psychology has evolved in the past decade, and the role of brand in this new Wild West consumer landscape. And armed with this intel, you'll never look at what it means to launch a business—or at your personal product obsessions—the same way again.

OBSESSED

1

FEAR OF DEATH

THE OTHER DAY, MY WIFE, JESS, WANDERED THROUGH OUR apartment opening kitchen cupboards and medicine cabinets, looking at product after product from brands that had all launched within the past few years. From our Goby electric toothbrushes to our Colugo stroller to multiple pairs of Allbirds shoes lined up by the door, our house had become a showroom for new business (not to mention a who's who of Red Antler clients).

Jess turned and asked, "Is there an end to all this? Will people at some point just run out of startup ideas?"

"Let's hope not," I said, "if we want Red Antler to stay in business!" But I'm not worried. After all, think about every purchase you've made in the past year. Was everything as affordable as it could be? Convenient as it could be? Was the packaging as innovative and sustainable as it could be? Was the experience as delightful as it could be?

As long as there are shortcomings or pain points, there's space for disruption. There's always a better, smarter, more humane way. The companies that are succeeding today are the ones who identify these issues and see them as opportunities. They recognize the blind spots, shortcomings, and failures of the old guard, and they're finding new, creative ways to solve problems for consumers. Problems are the most effective springboard for innovation.

Q: What does a book about branding have to do with "fear of death"?

Don't worry, this chapter is not about getting crushed under a mountain of Amazon boxes. It's about the most fundamental principle of building a beloved brand today, which is tapping into a real need for your consumers. I'll get to the death part in a bit. But first, a bit of background on how we got here.

A BRAND-NEW ERA

When we started Red Antler in 2007, "brand" was only just starting to get on the radar of entrepreneurs as something that needed their focus. "Design" was very much in the conversation as something startups should pay attention to, but for many that still meant user experience design, not brand design.*

Back in the ancient times at the start of the new millennium, great user experience design, or UX, was a meaningful competitive advantage. If something was easy to use, if it functioned beautifully, that was enough to get people excited. Google is the ultimate example of a business that launched at a specific point in time, with true and meaningful technological superiority, innovative UX, and a brand that almost seemed purposefully nonexistent. Its search results were just smarter (so smart they would give you only one result if you were "feeling lucky"!). Gmail was just easier. But if Google were to launch today, it would have to follow a different playbook. Uber is another company that got very far with mind-blowing technology and a user experience that felt like nothing that had come before. It frankly felt like magic, and at the time, that was enough. But even with all its success, Uber made itself vulnerable to Lyft and other competitors by not approaching brand through the right principles.

Regardless, most businesses are not Google or Uber. I am here to tell you that it is very, very unlikely you are sitting on the next

---

*In the simplest of terms, user experience design, or UX, most commonly refers to the design of a digital experience. Think about when you arrive at a website or open an app—what are the first things you see? How do you find your way around? How are you guided from one step to the next? Where do you need to touch or click or swipe? How are different features prioritized and arranged? Is how you use it intuitive? UX is an unbelievably important discipline, and it's nearly impossible to have a successful digitally led business without stellar user experience design. It's also a very important piece of the puzzle when we talk about branding. But on its own, it's not enough.

Google, in the same way that your college band was probably not the next Beatles. But that's okay! It is so unbelievably rare these days for a business to be meaningfully differentiated through its technology, or even its UX, alone. Once in a while, you'll see a company introduce a significant innovation, like dating app Tinder's swipe functionality, but it's only a matter of time before competitors copy it and the distinction simply starts to matter less. In most cases, UX is now more about elegance and simplicity than a major overhaul of how people are accustomed to having things function.

Q: If tech's not enough, and UX isn't enough, how do I differentiate?

That's where brand comes in. This does not mean you get to slap a cool logo on the top of your website and call it a day. Brand is not a logo, it's not your name, it's not a tagline. All of those things are important expressions of your brand, but they are only effective if you've done the hard work of figuring out what your brand stands for and why it matters in the first place. Just as tech and UX are not enough, "branding" in the traditional sense of the word is also not enough. At Red Antler, we aren't interested in working with businesses that want to create a "better brand" but don't offer any meaningful improvement on what exists today—as if brand is just about your colors and your copywriting. People come to us with these kinds of ideas all the time, pitching copycat businesses that have no good answer to the question "What makes you different?" yet think branding will make them stand out and succeed.

We also get approached by legacy businesses that want to compete with emerging challengers by creating a more appealing brand identity, but that aren't changing anything fundamental about the business itself. For example, we've had conversations with multi-decades-old retailers hoping to compete with e-commerce businesses. They want a new "brand identity" but don't want to invest in changing their physical spaces. They fail to realize that their stores are an inherent part of their identity and could even be a selling point compared to e-commerce. You can't have a conversation about brand today that doesn't start with the overall experience.

To build a winning brand today, you have to start with your customer and the problem you are solving for them. The brands that people love most are embedded within the business idea itself. Among the next generation of leading businesses, the best are thinking about their brand's purpose before they even launch. They seek to create a better experience that starts with their business model and extends to how they communicate and behave. Business model, tech, UX, brand experience—there's no clear delineation of these different elements; they all work together. And it all needs to be in service of the people you're trying to reach, because the consumer has never had more power or more say.

SOLVING A REAL PROBLEM

Whenever we kick off a new project with entrepreneurs, it always starts with a conversation. This is a chance for us to ask a million questions, get into their heads, understand their business and their vision, and tease out the points that are actually going to matter as we build a brand together. Founders don't struggle with a lack of ideas for what they're trying to achieve—usually it's that they know too much. A good founder can talk for hours about why what they're building is better in every way than anything out there (and ultimately how what they're really doing is changing the world!), and sometimes that's even true. The problem is that you can have an amazing product, and a big vision, but without a focus on brand from the beginning, it's going to fall flat. Today, nothing could be further from reality than "if you build it, they will come." That may have been true in the early days of the internet, when people were just so excited that they could buy [whatever] online, or that an app could do [that]. Those were the days when a new technology or an innovative business model was actually a meaningful point of difference, and you were able to launch with very little focus on brand and still gain traction.

The single most important question we ask in our first conversation with founders is not how their business works, or who their competition is, but what the problem is that they are solving for people. What I find amazing is that ninety-nine times out of one hundred, they don't answer with the problem they're solving—they answer with a description of their business and its benefit. Someone launching a new gym concept will answer, "Getting consistent quality training at an affordable price." Or someone launching a platform for small-business owners will say, "Visibility and ownership of their data." Notice these are not problems, these are solutions. It's very natural to jump to the solution—after all, when you're launching a business, that's what you spend all your time thinking about and working on. But to build a beloved brand from day one, it needs to be the opposite. You need to spend all your time thinking about the people you're hoping to reach, and how you intend to make their lives better.

When I used to work in advertising, my job was to write creative briefs, which is a sheet of paper that describes what the ad campaign needs to achieve. There's a section on the brief called the "consumer insight," which is supposed to contain a truth about the consumer that the agency would build the campaign around—what do we know about our target audience that should guide what we say to them? The example of a bad insight was "people wish there were a crunchy cereal with nuts and raisins." This is a bad insight, because it isn't true: people are *not* sitting around wishing for your exact cereal. They might want to lose weight, or maybe they get hungry again every day by 10:00 a.m., or maybe they're worried about heart health. But that doesn't mean they're wishing for your cereal. It's your job to show them how your cereal can be a solution to whatever problem it is they're facing.

Today, when we're building brands at Red Antler, we also start by thinking about the consumer insight, or the problem you're solving for people. Coming out of our conversation with founders, we first deliver the brand strategy, which is a document that outlines a vision for what the brand stands for, and we are usually creating it before the business has even launched. At the heart of this document are three critical pieces:

1. The mind-set of our target audience, meaning, who are the people this business is most for? This section is less about identifying an exact demographic (e.g., women in their midthirties living in major urban areas)

and more about identifying the attitudes and behaviors that define the people who will care about this brand the most. It's meant to paint a vivid picture of the "brand champion," the person who will be first to love the brand and will then spread the word.

2. The key problem for that audience, i.e., what's missing from their lives. Of everything we know about them, what's the most salient problem that this business can solve?

3. The brand idea, which shows how the brand is going to be the answer to this specific problem. This is a clear, singular statement about what the brand stands for at its core. It's the explanation of why this brand will matter to people.

3, the brand idea, becomes the foundation that drives all communication. But you cannot even begin to think about 3 until you are clear on 1 and 2. It doesn't matter what you think you stand for if it's not going to be relevant to anyone outside you and your team.

Q: Do I need to go through all this trouble if I'm sitting on an amazing new idea that's going to just blow people's minds the second they hear about it?

Um, yes. It's even more important to ground yourself in the problem you're solving when you're creating something new. The challenge at the heart of every innovation is that "new" is both your greatest advantage and your biggest liability. "New" gives you a reason for being, it's your something-to-talk-about, it's why press will write about you, it's why you should bother launching a business in the first place—but it's not necessarily why people will care, and that's the key distinction. When we're building brands for startups, we're helping solve the challenge of how to get people to care.

In fact, a fair definition of how to think about "brand" is "why should people care?" Sure, there's a subset of people who get excited about whatever's new. These are our early adopters, and startups would be lost without them. Early adopters pay attention to what's launching, they want the latest and greatest, and they'll be the first to tell their friends and rack up those referral program dollars. But you cannot scale a business on early adopters alone, and for the rest of the population, "new" is kinda uncomfortable. Even in our age of innovation, people aren't so automatically psyched about major changes to their daily lives. Modest improvements, sign me up! But a massive overhaul of how I do things? That sounds . . . hard. And maybe even scary.

That's why, as tempting as it is, you can't assume people are sitting around wishing your business existed. There's that famous Henry Ford quote (there's actually no evidence he ever said it, but you've all heard it), "If I had asked people what they wanted, they would have said faster horses." I recently heard the Steve Jobs version—swap out horses for typewriters. These quotes are typically employed to illustrate the shortcomings of relying too heavily on consumer research, and I wholeheartedly agree that you should not expect your consumers to tell you the answer. But that's not because your consumer doesn't matter. I've heard these quotes used to dismiss the importance of the consumer, in a haughty kind of way— "These sheep people have no idea what they want or need, so we'll just tell them! Mwah ha ha [rubs hands together maniacally]." But entrepreneurs who think this way have got it backward. It's not that people don't know what they want. The reason they would ask for a faster horse or a faster typewriter is because they have better things to do than sit around imagining far-flung inventions that will solve their problems, or wait for you to appear and solve it for them. They haven't even conceived of you, so you're going to have to work harder to build a connection. It's not enough to show up.

GETTING TO THE CONSUMER NEED

When I think about the most successful new brands of today, their successes have not come from convincing people of a new set of needs. Instead, they've introduced new, creative solutions to needs that are as old as time. In his 2004 book *The Seven Basic Plots*, Christopher Booker argues that every work of fiction can be categorized by seven plots—that there are only seven plots in the entire universe of stories, and every story fits into one of them. Perhaps the same can be said for consumer needs. On the surface, a business exists to solve a functional problem. Toothpaste exists because people need to clean their teeth or they'll fall out. Airplanes exist because people want to travel long distances in a short amount of time. But underneath these functional needs are core drivers, the universal things that people care about. All the best brands tap into these deeper human needs, beyond the functional, in one way or another. To build a brand that people truly fall in love with, that goes beyond a practical solution and actually becomes a valued part of their lives, you have to identify more than just the obvious need (or needs) you're answering. That's why whenever we sit down to build a brand, we start by identifying the problem the business is solving that is deeper than the obvious.

We do this by employing a method I call the "why test." Have you ever spent time with a toddler who keeps asking why, no matter what response you give? It's time to channel that toddler. And in honor of Henry Ford's fake quote, let's travel back in time and imagine ourselves as nineteenth-century entrepreneurs, wearing that era's equivalent of a hoodie, perhaps a mid-length sack coat, which according to Wikipedia replaced the frock coat for less formal occasions. And, exciting news, you just invented the car! Pretty amazing, right? Take a moment to congratulate yourself and fantasize about your valuation. You have this incredible innovation on your hands, and before you build a brand for it, you need to figure out what problem you're solving. And remember, it's not "people want a personal motorized way to get from point A to point B." That would be your version of the bad insight, the "people want a crunchy cereal with raisins." Instead, let's start with the obvious problem that people are facing in their daily lives. Perhaps it's something like "I rely on my horse to get around, but horses are slow, and they get tired." But don't stop there. This is where you employ the why test:

THE WHY TEST

Why does it matter to people that their horses are slow?

"It takes me too long to get places and I can't travel very far."

And why does that matter?

"I spend more time getting myself places than enjoying my life and accomplishing things."

And why does that matter?

"Because I'm going to die pretty soon and I have so much I need to achieve first! I can't waste my short life on the back of this horse!"

And there you go. The why test always ends with fear of death! Fear of death is the indicator that you've reached the end of the "why" chain. That's because everything we do as humans, whether we know it or not, is ultimately motivated by knowledge of our own mortality.

Now, not every brand needs to be built around fear of death. That might lead us to a place that's a little grim if you're trying to sell shoes or makeup, though it may make sense for healthcare. So maybe in our car example it's about the need to feel you're achieving enough, and that any time spent getting places is time not spent doing things you'd rather be doing. Or maybe it's about a need for freedom, and not wanting to be held back by constraints of distance. Before we even think about what a brand should stand for, we always make sure we're clear on the emotional need of our target audience. This ensures that any decisions we're making for the brand are actually going to be relevant for the people we're trying to reach. This is where consumer research plays a valuable role. You shouldn't expect that consumers are going to tell you word for word what your brand should stand for. But by listening closely, you can use research to determine what they're missing, and what they're struggling with.

When we helped create the brand for Keeps, a company that provides hair-loss solutions to men, we all went into the project certain that we'd be tapping into the loss of confidence that accompanies balding. Keeps was the first brand we launched with Thirty Madison, a new health company with the mission to bring specialized care and treatment to everyone. Thirty Madison's founders, Steve Gutentag and Demetri Karagas, both had personal experiences of realizing their hair was thinning, and dealing with the subsequent stress and confusion of trying to find solutions that worked in a category filled with false promises and snake oil (including scary potions that might actually be made of snake oil). Their mission was to help people overcome the stigma of hair loss, and give men everywhere access to both prescription and over-the-counter solutions that are proven to be effective. And the medications do work, but you have to start early—you can keep the hair you have, but you can't grow back what you've lost.

A big part of the business strategy was to target younger men, and get people using these treatments when they can still actually have an impact. Our hypothesis was that young men avoided treat-

ing their hair loss because they were embarrassed, especially because
the existing businesses were all targeting older men, with brands that
were extremely dated and cheesy (anyone remember "I'm not only
the Hair Club president, but I'm also a client"?). So we started talking to guys who were losing their hair but hadn't yet done anything
about it, and yes, there was certainly a level of embarrassment, and
stigma, and a lot of fear about going bald. But we also uncovered a
problem that hadn't occurred to us: many men were extremely reluc-
tant to treat any problem that wasn't an absolute emergency. They
won't go to the doctor unless their arm is on fire, they won't ask for
directions unless they . . . no, there's actually no circumstance in
which they'll ask for directions. We heard from a lot of guys some
version of "I know my hair is thinning, and I don't want to go bald,
but I'm going to wait until it's a real problem before I do something
about it." But of course, at that point, it's too late. This consumer
insight—a reluctance to ask for help for fear of seeming vulnerable
(vulnerability being a first cousin of "fear of death")—led us to our
brand strategy. If seeking help made men feel vulnerable, could we
flip the script, and instead show that taking action was something to
be proud of, not to fear? This led us to the idea of proactivity as a
point of pride: you're the kind of guy who gets things done.

Our strategic idea, "for the man of action," inspired us to build a
brand that celebrated taking control. Treating your hair loss is not
a sign of weakness—it's a sign that you're on top of it, that you're
getting ahead of the problem. Our brand idea was directly inspired
by our consumer insight. At no point did we consider building
the brand around a desire to save money, even though Keeps is more

affordable than other solutions, or a need for convenience, even though the whole thing happens online from the comfort of your home, including the doctor's consultation. These functional benefits are part of what the brand communicates, but they are not the brand idea. That's why it's so important to move beyond the obvious or the mundane when you think about what problem you're solving for people.

The consumer need and the brand idea are two sides of the same coin. The consumer need identifies the problem; the brand idea (which is intimately linked to the business idea) is the solution. Start with a need that's too small or functional, and you'll end with a brand idea that's lackluster, indefensible, and uninspiring. The problem you're solving is the foundation for your brand strategy, so you want to make sure you're setting yourself up to build a brand that taps into people's deepest motivations, dreams, and desires. And because these are deep, universal needs, they sometimes may feel obvious or familiar. Fear of failure. A need for self-expression. A desire to belong. It's okay that a lot of brands tap into the same themes. In fact, if you're introducing a new idea to the world, grounding it in a familiar need is important. "You've always felt this way, and here's a new solution." Familiar problem, unexpected answer. It's that combination of comfort and surprise that enables new brands to so quickly make their way into people's lives and become indispensable. Instead of seeming like a risky, scary new invention that's asking people to change their behavior in a way they're not sure they're ready for, it's the answer they've been waiting for all along. They just didn't know it yet.

AIRBNB'S BRAND JOURNEY

When you launch an idea into the world, brand is the driving force that helps people understand how this new business fits into their lives, and why they should care. In an ideal scenario, this work is happening before launch, smoothing the path to mass adoption and creating a sense of connection from day one. Not only can rebrands be costly and time consuming, but there's the risk you won't even get the chance to rebrand if you don't have enough momentum out of the gate, which is why companies launching today should strive to get it right from the start. However, the entrepreneurial journey is never straightforward, and some businesses only find their way after they launch, taking a longer and more meandering path to reveal their purpose. Airbnb is a great example of a business that was very ahead of its time, but it struggled to gain traction until its founders were able to crystallize the exact problem they were solving for people. Founders Brian Chesky and Joe Gebbia, two designers living in San Francisco, came up with the idea for the business quite organically in 2007. They were struggling to make rent, a design conference was coming to town and as usual every hotel room in San Francisco was booked, and they had the idea to earn some extra cash by renting out space in their apartment, specifically three air mattresses in their spare bedroom. The thought of posting on Craigslist seemed too impersonal, so they put up their own website, originally called airbedandbreakfast.com, to facilitate the process.

It would be tempting now to just say, "And the rest is history." But their path to growth was not a straight shot to the top, and there were multiple junctures at which they were at risk of failing alto-gether. People didn't automatically take to the idea of staying in other people's houses, particularly the earliest iteration in which the own-ers of the house were always meant to be present. And investors didn't get it right away either—as two designers, with no technical cofounder, and an idea that was not an obvious home run, Chesky and Gebbia struggled to raise money in those early days. But their journey of growing their business was simultaneously a journey of defining their brand, and the deeper they went on what their brand really meant to people, the more success they saw. Airbnb has noth-ing to complain about now, but it's entirely possible that growth would have come more easily had Airbnb launched with a clearer articulation of its purpose from the beginning.

In the first couple of years, Chesky and Gebbia made some prac-tical and also some highly imaginative moves that helped them along their way. In 2008, they created and sold election-themed limited edition cereal boxes to pay off the debt they had incurred starting the business (and miraculously sold $30,000 worth of Obama O's and Cap'n McCain's). That year they also made it into famous tech incu-bator Y Combinator, which came with $20,000 in seed funding, and in the process brought on third founder Nathan Blecharczyk, who had a technical background. Next, from talking to users, they dis-covered that a major barrier to using the site was that the listings didn't look appealing. So they took the initiative to visit a bunch of host apartments in New York City and take pictures themselves. In 2010 they enticed a bunch of people over from Craigslist to post on their site instead, creating a bot that grabbed information from Craigslist listings and automatically forwarded the newly created listing to users for easy publishing. In 2012 they redesigned their site and app and launched a "Wish List" feature that enabled users to collect their favorite Airbnb destinations into themed groups. A ton has been written on the amazing and unlikely path to growth of Airbnb, and it's a great story that involves a lot of swing-for-the-fences moments, determination, and certainly a bit of luck. But the founders ultimately credit their success to gaining an understanding of what their business actually meant to people.

By 2013, Airbnb had built an impressively large community of passionate users, and had raised their Series C in funding. The more they talked to their own community, including nearly five hundred interviews their team conducted with people around the world, the more the same word kept coming up: *belonging*. The problem that Airbnb solves for people is not offering a cheap place to stay when all the hotels in San Francisco are sold out for a conference. It's that when people travel, they don't want to feel like tourists or outsiders. They want to have a deeper experience of the place. They want to spend their time meaningfully, because time of course is limited. And that's what Airbnb offers: whether or not the host is home (because the business naturally evolved to a state where most people are renting empty houses and apartments, not crashing on couches), it's a different experience staying in a real person's home versus a hotel room. You're more likely to stay in a less touristy neighborhood. You're more likely to get a flavor of the local culture. You're less likely to feel like a stranger in a strange land, because you're "in." You have the insider's view. Let's imagine the why test for Airbnb, shall we?

WHAT'S THE PROBLEM THAT AIRBNB IS SOLVING?

- Not only are hotels overpriced—they are generic and unspecial.

Why does that matter?

- People don't want to feel like tourists when they visit a new place; they want to see it like the locals do.

Why does that matter?

- Because they want to have authentic experiences, not manufactured ones. They want to feel they're genuinely experiencing a place from within, not as an outsider.

Why does that matter?

- Because they travel to make their lives richer.

Why does that matter?

- Because the moments we remember are not the mundane ones in front of a computer or doing laundry, but the ones when we truly feel a part of something, where we belong to something bigger.

Why does that matter?

- Because we're all going to die!

People all want to belong, and that's what Airbnb solves for people. The problem is solved in the business model itself, as well as in the way Airbnb continuously engages with its community. From the early days, it employed the strategy of meeting up with users in person, getting direct feedback, and demonstrating a genuine commitment to building a real-life community, not just using *community* as a buzzword to describe its social media following. As the business expanded internationally, it had a harder time growing the "supply side" than the demand side, because people aren't always comfortable opening up their homes. It solved this challenge by sending small teams of people to new markets, to host parties and information sessions, engaging in face-to-face conversations with potential hosts. Even though at a glance this tactic was not the most scalable, Airbnb grew two times faster in the markets it entered with a human presence. This was a business that was about solving the need for human connection, and by leaning into that idea, it grew more quickly.

In 2014, Airbnb underwent a brand evolution to fully embody this idea of "belonging" that had been at the heart of the brand all along, even before it had been explicitly articulated. It created a new logo, which included a symbol nicknamed the Bélo, meant to represent the coming together of people, places, love, and Airbnb itself. Airbnb changed its tagline from "Travel like a Human" to "Belong Anywhere" because the brand is more than a tool for travel, it's about helping people feel at home all across the world. It moved its color from "startup blue" (not its technical name) to a more passionate, nurturing pink red. Airbnb went a little overboard with its communication of the rebrand, releasing a video explaining its thinking and process, and naming its new symbol. Consumers don't need to be told every detail of why a company makes brand decisions, as long as the effects can be felt. But the intention behind the move was powerful: finally able to articulate the deeper problem it was solving for people, Airbnb evolved its identity to better express the brand's purpose. Airbnb didn't succeed because of its new logo—by the time it rebranded, it had raised its Series D and was seeing hundreds of millions of dollars in annual revenue. The brand already existed, if you think of brand as "why should people care." It was time for the identity to catch up.

Airbnb's well-defined sense of the problem it's solving for its users continues to fold back into the product itself. In 2016, it announced the launch of Experiences, a new platform that allows people to book experiences hosted by locals, from cooking classes in someone's home, to a hike, to a jazz club tour. Airbnb Experiences takes the idea of belonging to the next level, empowering hosts to share a slice of their hometown through the lens of their passion or expertise, and of course enabling travelers or even locals to see a side of a place they would never otherwise have access to. And the design language of the brand has continued to evolve too. In 2018, Airbnb worked with famed type foundry Dalton Maag to create a custom font called Cereal, which was flexible enough to be used across marketing channels and within the product itself, and could be extended across the many different languages and alphabets of Airbnb's global community. Most brands have a set of typefaces that they use in different circumstances: one for large headlines, another for interactions on their website. By creating one typeface that can be used in all circumstances, Airbnb reinforces the ideas of unity and belonging—even its font belongs anywhere.

Q: Do I have to create an entirely new business model to have a unique brand?

What's most interesting about Airbnb's success is that its business model wasn't even entirely new. HomeAway launched in 2004, and Vrbo, now owned by HomeAway, had been around since the '90s (the '90s!!!). But both sites were and still are very transactional, stripping out the human side of their offerings and instead focusing on the properties. The properties are presented in a way that feels simply like an alternative to a hotel room—but with a kitchen!—rather than a chance to have a more local, special kind of experience. Again, the problem that Airbnb is solving isn't that hotels are too expensive, or that hotel rooms don't have kitchens and laundry. Or rather, yes, it is solving those problems, but it also taps into a deeper, more human need. By tapping into a true need, Airbnb has been able to completely redefine a category for people across the world, and saw over $1 billion in revenue in just one quarter of 2018. It has elevated the brand beyond a cheap, potentially even sketchy-sounding, place to stay to the best possible way to experience a locale.

As demonstrated by the launch of Airbnb's Experiences feature, a deeper sense of a brand's reason for being doesn't just influence communications but can unlock opportunities within the product itself, which is just as much a part of brand as a logo or an ad campaign. Think about the love for Venmo, an app that launched to facilitate the easy transfer of money. There was no shortage of ways to exchange money before Venmo, including PayPal, now its parent company. There's arguably nothing more functional or transactional than an app that's literally designed for financial transactions. But Venmo rose to success by becoming not a business-to-business brand but a beloved consumer brand in a way that nothing in its space had before. The problem that Venmo solved for people is that asking your friends for money is sort of awkward. And if you're out socializing, or having fun, or sharing experiences, the last thing you want to do is introduce finances into the equation. Venmo turned this tension on its head by transforming the financial exchange into a social moment. By requiring its users to list a reason for payment, and by introducing fun emojis into the mix, Venmo created a public social feed that's a form of entertainment in itself. Scrolling through the Venmo feed reveals all sorts of tantalizing details about your network—who's hanging out with whom, who's coming up with clever synonyms that clearly mean drugs, which couples have a very strange approach to joint finances. Suddenly, paying someone back becomes a chance to display your wit and broadcast good times together, rather than something to be a little embarrassed about (or avoid doing altogether).

What these beloved brands do so successfully is make it about the consumer, not themselves. Airbnb grew in service of its community. It dug deep into the problem it was solving for people, and oriented its business and brand around continuing to solve that problem in new and surprising ways. When you ground yourself in your consumers and why you exist for them, branding becomes an act of generosity instead of an act of self-congratulation. It's not about "look at me, listen to me, this is why I'm wonderful, pay attention." Instead, it's "here's what I understand about your needs, and here's how I'm here to help." Every time you ask for the attention of your consumers, it's to tell them something that serves them. Every time you conceive of a new feature, it's to better tap into their existing desires. There's a justification for innovation that's rooted in actually solving real problems, not just new for newness' sake. To successfully launch something new and have people fall in love with it, you need to tap into a need that's deep and true, and that has existed for a long time before you came on the scene, perhaps as primal as fear of death itself. Then and only then can you show why you're worthy of obsession.

> *Remember:* Once you think you've identified the absolute deepest consumer problem that your business is solving, go a level deeper! Work to identify the need behind the need.

2

ELEVATE TO THE EMOTIONAL

BEFORE I STARTED RED ANTLER, MY LAST JOB IN ADVERtising was working on the world's leading diamond brand. It was such an exciting change for me. Prior to that, I had worked mostly on CPG food brands. CPG stands for "consumer packaged goods"—in other words, stuff that's sold in boxes in grocery stores. As much as food represents a primal need, packaged goods advertising rarely broke away from functional messaging. More or less every strategy was a version of "it's an easy way to feed your family a healthy meal!" Or, when I started working on a yogurt account, "it's a delicious way to feed yourself a healthy snack!"

But advertising diamonds was the opposite. Let's be honest: there is zero functional benefit to a diamond (unless you are a jewel thief who needs to cut your way through a sheet of glass to escape). We could only tell emotional stories. I got to travel around the country and talk to people about their deepest hopes and fears as they related to love, and then figure out how to imbue those feelings into a very expensive, albeit beautiful, stone. I had gone from one extreme to the other, which is fortunate because in today's world, brands need to do it all. When you are launching a new product, you can't stick to the rational, or be purely emotional. You need to find a way to bring the two together, thinking not just about what a brand does or what it says, but how it makes people feel.

FEATURES MATTER, BUT THEY'RE NOT ENOUGH

Lately, I've been hearing a lot of variations on the idea that "brand is the most important thing" or that "brand is all that really matters when you're launching a business." Obviously, as someone who runs a brand company, I'm not sad that people are starting to notice the important role that brand plays. But we're witnessing a too extreme swing of the pendulum—it used to be that entrepreneurs didn't think brand mattered at all if they had a stellar product; now people think brand is a magic bullet. The truth is that neither is true. You can't isolate "brand" from the business. This type of thinking, "all that matters is the brand," implies that branding is a shiny layer that sits on top of a product, convincing people whatever you're selling is worthwhile. And, sure, if you have an appealing aesthetic, and smart copywriting, that may be enough to get people's attention and get them to try something. But if they start to dig in and there's nothing underneath, if your product doesn't deliver on your promise, they aren't going to come back for more, and they certainly aren't going to become your champions.

As I discussed in chapter 1, the first step is identifying the true problem you are solving for people, beyond the obvious. That sets you up to build a brand that's deeply relevant to the people you want to reach. The next step, which I'll cover in this chapter, is determining the emotional territory that your brand will occupy in people's lives; in other words, how your brand will make them feel. But before you can have a conversation about the emotional resonance of a brand, you have to start with the product itself. With very few exceptions, the product needs to have meaningful differentiation in order to build a brand that people love. At Red Antler, we often meet entrepreneurs who are looking to launch a business that's just like everything else, and they are hoping that we can help them stand out from the competition with a unique brand. We politely pass on those opportunities. Sometimes founders are taken aback when we push to understand what makes their business different from its competitors, or how it will benefit people, thinking that it's our job to figure out how to make a business seem different, whether or not it actually is. We'll ask, "What makes these [socks, bras, snacks, you name it] different?" And they'll say, "That's where you come in!" But great branding needs to start from the inside and work its way out. You need to understand what's special about the business and then figure out how to take what's special and elevate it to a story with emotional resonance. When I'm creating a brand's strategy, I don't just make it up or pull it from thin air. I go deep into a business's reasons for being, and craft a story that flows naturally out of the product's benefits.

Q: How do I balance communicating product benefits with telling an emotional story?

You can't think of the benefits of the product and the feelings of the brand as two separate things that need to be "balanced." Instead, you need to figure out how to connect them. Every product has a set of functional benefits. Most business ideas start with a focus on the functional benefits and, ideally, an aim to improve upon what's already out there. It's going to be cheaper. More convenient. More comfortable. Better fit. Better customer service. A simpler shopping experience. It will taste amazing. It's healthy. It helps you get organized. It helps you make more money. These benefits are deeply important to the success of a business, but they are not the be-all and end-all of your brand strategy. If you think back to the why test and how you need to dig deeper until you get to the real problem you're solving for people, you can do the same for benefits, only going in the opposite direction. Start with your functional benefits, the full set of them, and then figure out how they can all build to an overarching emotional territory, in other words, how the brand will make people feel. These days, the most successful brands do not simply invent an emotional idea that has no basis in their product benefits. Historically, TV commercials often told stories that had little to no connection to the products they were selling: they simply aimed to get a laugh or a cry, while reminding you that Doritos or AT&T exists (like we could ever forget you, Doritos!). But to build a brand today that people love from day one, there needs to be a clear through line, meaning that the story that brands tell and the feelings they evoke should be supported by what the product actually does. You've likely had a conversation about branding where someone brings up "authenticity" (lucky you if it was just once). One of the surest ways to guarantee that coveted authenticity is to make sure that whatever you're claiming as your brand's higher-order purpose actually aligns with what your product does. Your brand strategy is rooted in an emotional idea, but it's an idea that's supported by your functional benefits. .

The idea of elevating to a feeling or emotion is not new. In fact, it's been a core principle of branding and advertising since the beginning of consumerism. Think about Coca-Cola standing for happiness, or Marlboro standing for masculine coolness. What's new about the brands launching today is that their emotional story is far more closely tied to what their products actually do and how they behave. The positive feelings don't stop at the end of the commercial. The brand idea extends throughout the entire experience, from customer service to packaging to the product itself. Brand can no longer be a layer that sits on top of whatever you're selling, weaving a false narrative about what you offer people. We're no longer living in a time where you can convince people that a can of bubbly sugar water stands for "youth" or "happiness." Consumers are too educated these days. They have far too many choices, and their expectations are too high to get away with "shallow branding." Just consider the backlash faced by Gillette, the shaving brand, when they launched a very buzzy commercial attacking toxic masculinity in 2019. I'm not talking about the men who were outraged by what they perceived as an attack on them, because they aren't even worth the strain on my keyboard. But other consumers rightly pointed out the hypocrisy of a brand that claims to stand for feminism in its communications but still charges a "pink tax," i.e., a surcharge for identical razors that happen to be marketed to women. It's not enough to publicly stand for feminism—you have to walk the walk.

Q: Why do I even need to worry about an emotional story when I'm creating a brand? Wouldn't the most honest move be simply to say, "This is a toothbrush. It's cheaper, and it works better than other toothbrushes. Decide for yourself."

The problem with focusing solely on your functional benefits is that they aren't enough to get people to care, let alone to inspire love from day one. Even though they are critical, they are also likely table stakes. It would be foolish to launch a business these days that isn't quicker, or cheaper, or smarter, because if you aren't improving on the status quo, there's little reason for you to launch in the first place. Most of the businesses we've helped launch at Red Antler—Colugo strollers, Casper mattresses, Keeps hair loss, Snowe housewares, I could go on—offers a more affordable option that's the same quality as the premium legacy products already on the market. And not one of these brands is built on the idea of helping people save money.

That doesn't mean we don't talk about price anywhere—there's a time and a place to highlight affordability. But if you build a brand that stands for affordability alone, anyone can come along, be five dollars cheaper, and you're done. The same goes for price's equally boring cousin, convenience. Every brand these days offers convenience. There are way too many ad campaigns for startups that are all some version of "you have better things to do, so we take care of *x* for you." That idea is not unique.

Before you even think about trying to own convenience as your brand idea, I need to address the elephant in every room in every house. You probably saw this coming. Maybe you're even surprised I waited this long. I need to talk about Amazon. Amazon is so offensively convenient that it's pretty much impossible to go up against them on convenience alone. You simply aren't going to win that battle. But Amazon is also not the unassailable enemy that some people fear. I may regret putting this in writing when one day we're all working for Amazon or Amazon has a chip in my brain, but I do not believe that Amazon will eventually crush every business until it's all that remains. (Sorry, Amazon! I didn't mean it! I love you, Amazon!) And that's because all that Amazon stands for, when all is said and done, is convenience. It's not more delightful to shop on Amazon. Amazon doesn't help you discover amazing new things. Amazon doesn't make you feel much, other than "holy sh&t I can't believe how fast that got here." Just like many of you, I'm a little bit addicted to Amazon. I hope this is a safe space where I can admit that I order an embarrassing number of products each week. But the items that I'm ordering either are from brands I've fallen in love with elsewhere, or are so boring and functional I can't even be bothered to have a brand affinity (and in some of those cases, a new brand could easily come along and change my mind). It's not a place for discovery, or loyalty, or fun. It's a left-brain calculation. In fact, I pay more to buy books at my local bookstore, Books Are Magic in Brooklyn, because I love the experience of shopping there and I value its presence in my neighborhood.

That's why new brands are still able to launch and succeed, even with Amazon and its plucky sidekick Alexa infiltrating so much of our lives. These days more than ever, people want to feel an emotional connection to the things they buy and the places they shop. They want to feel something other than "that was fast." And that's why, even though it's hard to launch a business that isn't convenient, you can't stop there. You have to figure out what you're bringing people that goes beyond the rational. This isn't about deception or obfuscation. It's about recognizing that every time you are communicating with someone—whether that's through an ad, your website, a piece of direct mail, or most important, the experience of your product itself—you have the chance to make them feel something positive, or to make them feel nothing at all. Put another way, if you're asking people to spend time with you, shouldn't you make it worth their while? If you follow the rule of starting with the problem you're solving for people, then this isn't about tricking people into falling in love with you. It's about tapping into something they need and genuinely solving it for them, which is also why your product actually needs to deliver. When people accuse branding of being manipulative, that's not giving consumers enough credit. No one is going to be fooled by a cool logo. But they are going to be drawn to the brands that go out of their way to tell a more interesting, compelling, and meaning-ful story about why they exist in the world and then back that story up with a product experience that's better for people's lives.

HOW BOXED AND ALLBIRDS CONNECT THE FUNCTIONAL AND THE EMOTIONAL

You don't have to be selling diamonds to tell an emotionally reso-nant story. We worked with Boxed, a mobile-first retailer that sells everyday items in bulk, at wholesale prices. Think Costco, but digi-tally native. When we first met Boxed, it had already launched, and it was struggling to get out of the "Costco but more convenient and without the membership fee" trap. You never want to define your brand solely in relation to another brand ("it's Twitter meets Pin-terest with a touch of Uber"—not good). All of Boxed's early com-munications were about saving your Saturday from the trip to the wholesale club. Convenience is a huge part of the Boxed story, and our intention was never to abandon convenience in favor of an en-tirely new message. The brand still promises to give you your time back. But especially with a business liked Boxed, which is arguably a competitor to Amazon and sells many of the same items you can buy on Amazon, we had to figure out what the brand stood for be-yond convenience alone. By speaking directly with customers, we discovered that there's an emotional benefit to buying in bulk beyond just the cost or time savings. There's a feeling that comes from having a stocked closet or pantry, a feeling of preparedness and pride that you're ready for whatever life throws at you. Given their space constraints, some city dwellers probably have a harder time relating to this, but for people in most parts of the country, opening a closet that's filled with rolls upon rolls of toilet paper gives you a glowy sense of achievement—you are *ready*. This led us to our brand strategy of "all set for life." Before we conducted our consumer research, the Boxed team was hesitant to even use the word *bulk*, because they feared it sounded cheap or unappealing. But our new strategy gave us permission to lean into bulk as part of the brand story. We created a new logo that was bold and chunky, and new lines for the brand that included "Love That Bulk," and "Don't Run Out" (which obviously plays on the idea of convenience—you don't need to run out to the store—but also our positive emotional feeling of never running out of the things you need). Boxed still communicates about saving your Saturday, but it does so with a strong, ownable point of view that isn't about convenience alone.

The brands that people love the most all stand for a clear emotional idea that's greater than the product's benefits. When we start working with a company, we start with the problem we're solving for people, and the next step is to define the idea a brand stands for, and how the brand should make people feel. Only once we have that idea do we start to think about tonality, design, language. Everything that a brand does and everything that a consumer experiences is influenced by this core idea. That doesn't mean we're always overtly expressing it—sometimes you just need to explain what a thing is or how it works. Sometimes you need to tout a product's functional benefits. But the emotional idea is always there, influencing our decisions, guiding how the brand behaves. There's the product and what it does, and then there's what the brand stands for.

When we first met the founders of Allbirds, Joey Zwillinger and Tim Brown, we were blown away by their product story. Tim had spent nearly a decade playing professional football (soccer for the Americans in the room), for the New Zealand national football team. During that time, he was gifted a lot of free shoes, and he became dismayed by the footwear industry after being sent product after product that was covered in logos and bright, flashy colors while made cheaply from some of the most environmentally damaging materials in the world. Hailing from New Zealand, Tim grew up witnessing firsthand the amazing powers of merino wool—a premium material that's not only soft, breathable, and temperature regulating, but grows back every year. He wondered why merino wool had never been used in footwear and decided to investigate the possibility of creating a new kind of shoe made from wool. After a period of R & D, Tim developed and patented a wool-based material that was strong and durable enough to be a shoe, but still soft and flexible. In March 2014, Tim launched a Kickstarter campaign to test demand for his Wool Runner. Hoping to raise $30,000, he had to shut down the campaign within four days after raising $120,000.

To make his vision a reality, Tim needed a partner who understood supply chains. Joey had been running the chemical division at a company called Solazyme, which used biotechnology to create microalgae that could metabolize sugar and convert it into renewable products. The two teamed up to create Allbirds, then called Three Over Seven, in early 2015. We met them that spring, roughly nine months before the public launch date. Even with the incredibly positive feedback from the Kickstarter community, the cofounders knew that a business could not successfully launch in this category without a serious focus on brand. After all, footwear is one of the most brand-led categories in the world. There's Nike, which, next to Apple, comes up most often in project kickoffs as everyone's most admired brand. Nike is so beloved that it's hard not to roll your eyes when people list it as their favorite brand. And yet, it's also hard to argue with that choice, because Nike does such a fantastic job in all its communication. Few brands are better at continually laddering up to an emotional idea and standing for more than just their products' benefits. Nike is never just about the shoes; it always ladders up to the idea of performance, that there's an athlete in all of us. And Nike has set the bar for every other shoe brand, arguably every other brand, to tell a bigger story about why people should care.

When Allbirds came to us, they had two compelling sides to their business. Both mattered deeply and would form the basis for creating a beloved, game-changing brand that could credibly stand for an emotional idea.

1. The Mission to Transform the Footwear Industry with a Focus on Sustainable Materials

This mission was at the heart of the brand's reason for being, and it was a major part of the story. But we all agreed that the brand would never have the reach and impact it was aiming for if it was positioned as the "environmental sneaker" alone. There would be a small subset of people who cared enough about the environment that they would buy a shoe solely (is that a shoe pun?) for that reason, and it would stop there. To reach a broader audience, Allbirds had to tell a story that emotionally related to people's lives and not just their desire to do good. It's true that people care more and more about a brand's social and environmental impact, and are drawn to brands that are doing good things for the world. So many brands today are looking to do well by doing good, whether it's in the materials they use, or the "buy one give one" model that Toms Shoes invented, or a connection with a cause. I hope the brands that are launching today understand that they can't just pay lip service to corporate responsibility—consumers have gotten too smart for that, and they can see through the fakers. If a social mission is not inherently connected to the business and brand story, it, too, can feel like a layer that just sits on top, something tacked on. It's encouraging that, like affordability and convenience, connection to a larger mission is slowly but surely becoming table stakes. I'm incredibly skeptical of the brands we meet who aren't thinking about sustainability as part of their product or packaging strategy, or who aren't focused on the larger impact they seek to have in the world. I hope the world is heading to a place where you can't launch a business without the aim of improving how things get made and done, to the benefit of people and the planet. Allbirds is certainly helping to set the bar, and I am by no means trying to minimize the importance or relevance of the brand's focus on sustainability. Without it, Allbirds would be just another shoe brand. But I would argue that sustainability falls more into the category of a "functional benefit" than a feeling. If you think back to grounding everything a brand does in the problem you're solving for people, you still need a brand story that connects to a deep human truth, one that's personally felt. Most people care about the environment, but they don't feel the earth's pain as their own (at least not yet).

2. The Shoe Itself

If the Allbirds shoe were not awesome, no amount of brand magic could have made up for it. The shoe was designed with a couple of core principles in mind. One was an adherence to minimalism, an antidote to the overbranded, logo-covered, bright and flashy sneakers that are mini walking billboards on your feet. The founders wanted a shoe designed for versatility: because of its minimalist design, you could wear it to the gym, to work, and out to dinner, and it would blend into all of these scenarios. The goal was to create a shoe that would allow you to pack for a trip and bring just the one pair. And the second principle was comfort. Now, I know what you're thinking. Aren't all sneakers designed to be comfortable? I don't want this to start sounding like an ad for Allbirds, but if you haven't tried them, you just have to trust me on this—these shoes are really, *really* comfortable. They're so comfortable that it actually becomes hard to wear other shoes after you get used to them. But comfort, though appealing, was potentially a curse. Other shoe brands that have leaned too much into comfort have become decidedly uncool. I won't name names, but you know those "mom sneaker" or "dad sneaker" brands. Comfort on its own is not the sexiest of attributes.

Allbirds had its benefits: sustainability, minimalist design, and comfort. And what the team discovered is that all three connect to the idea of exploration. The shoe itself enables you to go anywhere, with nothing holding you back: "One shoe for all you do." Throw them on, hop on a plane, see the world. And, of course, exploration also ties to the environmental mission—the company is constantly seeking new uses for the world's most sustainable materials, and reimagining how to make the things we own. Exploration became the umbrella idea connecting the business, the product, and the brand, which led to the emotional territory of "curiosity." Evoking a feeling of curiosity became the guiding light for creative decisions, starting with the name itself. The goal was to find a name that wasn't too literal or obvious, that would spark people's imagination. A group was sitting around, brainstorming ideas (or what we call "namestorming"), and someone asked, "What are some other birds from New Zealand that aren't the kiwi?" (Tim's home country of New Zealand is famous for the kiwi, and therefore it felt way too obvious.) Everyone liked the idea of tying the name to the brand's New Zealand roots, and birds as a symbol felt very connected to the strategy of exploration. One of the New Zealanders answered, "Well, before people arrived on New Zealand, it was all birds." Immediately, the image of this far-off island country filled with only birds struck everyone for its beauty and poignancy. Sometimes naming takes weeks and weeks of discarded ideas, but the second we heard that answer, we all knew the name had to be Allbirds. It was weird in just the right way, and not only that, there was a subtle environmental story, because once people arrived on New Zealand, they brought with them other animals and the ecosystem changed. It's a direct example of the impact of human presence on nature. But our intention was never to get into all of that. No one expected that consumers would know why the brand was called Allbirds. Tim and Joey liked that it was different, and that it made people a little uncomfortable, and, most important, it made people curious. It didn't sound like any other shoe brand.

Q: If my brand name doesn't communicate anything about my product, doesn't that mean I need to spend more time and effort explaining to consumers what it is?

The best brand names lean into a feeling instead of relying entirely on functional benefits. So many times, new brands try to create a name that describes exactly what they do. This is particularly true for brands that try to "test" their name ideas among consumers, because in the absence of any context, people are always drawn to the most literal, descriptive names. But in the real world, consumers are rarely, if ever, encountering a name out of context. A name is always seen in the context of other communication, so it's usually smarter to choose a name that's more emotional and abstract. Otherwise, on a purely practical level, you can end up in a situation where your business evolves (as most businesses do) and your name no longer encompasses your offering. I think of examples like overstock.com or Mailchimp, which had to run advertising campaigns explaining how their businesses do more than just what their names describe. What an enormous waste of a media budget that could be spent on communicating pretty much anything else about these businesses. Beyond the practical, a name is also an opportunity to evoke a feeling and pique curiosity, rather than simply stating what a business does. If your name tells people exactly what you're about, the conversation is over before it begins. It's Microsoft versus Apple. In nearly every case, we urge businesses not to worry about communicating their functional benefits, but instead to choose a name that we can build a feeling around. A name should be a canvas for the brand—there can be symbolic meaning, like Allbirds, or even a clearer connection to what the business does, like Lyft, but it should be open enough that it won't limit growth, and that people can embed their own meaning into it.

The name is also just the beginning, and just a piece of the branding puzzle. The visual and verbal world of the Allbirds brand was built with curiosity as the guiding light. It has a loose, scripty logo, inspired by shoelaces, that's extremely unusual for the category. Its icon is an abstract bird, created from the *s*, taking the unconventional approach of using the last letter of the name for the brand shorthand instead of the first. New Zealand–based illustrator Toby Morris created a whimsical, wonderful world of illustrations that invite people to explore. This includes the Allbirds "spokes-sheep" Peter, an animated sheep who appears in many of the brand's transactional emails to add unexpected joy to even the most functional communications, like an order confirmation. In every choice, All-

birds brings an element of surprise. The original e-commerce experience included subtle but noteworthy moments like a GIF depicting
toes wiggling in wool to give a visceral feeling of softness. All of the
initial photography showed people on the move, heading off frame
to their next adventure.

For the opening message on the site, a deceptively simple headline ended up becoming a defining part of the brand in its early days:
"Turns out, the world's most comfortable shoe is made of wool."
While on the surface this line appears to be as direct and straightforward as can be, the addition of *turns out* not only created a casual,
conversational tone, but also spoke to the discovery and innovation
that led to the shoe's creation. Allbirds took ownership of the idea of
the *world's most comfortable shoe*, a moniker that press then picked up
and that became the leading description of the brand. To improve
on the traditional box-within-a-box packaging, the team invented
a shoebox that could also serve as the shipping carton, an innovation
that led to a 40 percent reduction in cardboard. It also unfolded
like a book, creating a wonderful opportunity for brand storytelling.
In each of these moments, whether it's talking about comfort or re-
inforcing the business's commitment to sustainability, the brand creates
emotional resonance and generates the feeling of curiosity.

Allbirds has seen staggering success, and since launch has introduced new silhouettes and new materials, all made, of course, from
sustainable resources. Its team continues to take the brand to new
heights, opening physical retail stores, expanding into new countries,
and releasing limited edition colors that often sell out and keep people coming back for more. Sometimes it feels like everywhere you go,
someone's wearing Allbirds (even President Obama was spotted in a

pair). What makes me happiest is that even though some accuse Allbirds of being the unofficial uniform of the Silicon Valley tech world, my ninety-three-year-old grandma had a pair that she absolutely adored, and kids are running around in Smallbirds. There's a universality to the product and the brand that's due to the incredible comfort and versatility of the shoes themselves, as well as the emotional space the brand occupies. The positivity of the Allbirds brand is something that everyone can sign up for, which is not the same as trying to be all things to all people. Allbirds has a unique tonality and aesthetic, but its emotional territory transcends demographics or geographies. The brand's personality is rooted in an environmental mission that's easy to believe in but that is effective only because it's backed up by genuine innovation and products that do what they're supposed to do. The brand is not just entertaining—it's a vehicle for telling a meaningful story about the shoes and their purpose in the world, both at a macro level and the micro level of everyday comfort. Far from being a layer that sits on top, the brand narrative, the business purpose, and the product benefits of Allbirds are all intertwined with each other.

STANDING OUT FROM THE CROWD

Allbirds is a business with an amazing innovation story and incredible products, but ultimately the love people have for the brand is rooted in how it makes them feel. With innovative businesses, there's a risk of getting bogged down in the details, mistakenly believing that a new product story alone is enough to get people to care. But no matter how interesting or unique the product is, we are always thinking about how the brand can connect with people on a personal level. We faced this challenge with another client of ours, Bowery. Bowery is an indoor farming company that is aiming to solve the world's food crisis (no big deal) through its proprietary indoor growing process, which enables fresh produce to be grown pretty much anywhere, using 95 percent less water than traditional agriculture, and with one hundred times more productivity on the same footprint of land. It's a very exciting story, but the problem is that it directly flies in the face of what most people want to feel when they buy vegetables. People idealize farming as the exact opposite of innovation and technology—it's a "return to the land, hands in the dirt" vision of the days of yore. Working hand in hand with CEO Irving Fain, we set out to create a brand that would celebrate Bowery as "the modern farming company" but still tap into people's desires for fresh, natural produce, and the feeling that they were making the best possible choice for themselves and their families. It was never about hiding Bowery's methods, but instead linking them to the feeling we knew people were seeking.

We knew that consumers' gold standard for produce was local and organic. So we highlighted the fact that because Bowery's farms are indoors, they are as local as can be—produce can be grown just miles from where it's sold. As for organic, Bowery is able to grow its vegetables with zero pesticides because of its complete control over the growing environment, so it's actually better than organic. Bowery's precise control of the farming process leads to the purest produce imaginable. This unique blending of natural with precise defined our brand identity and guided our creative choices, enabling us to highlight innovation while still driving a feeling of comfort and nourishment. We celebrated contrast and surprise: you wouldn't expect the purest produce imaginable to be grown indoors, but it is. The brand's visual language contains loose, expressive forms that are created with a high degree of precision and craft. The name embraces contrast, too, and was a tough decision because "the Bowery" in New York does not exactly conjure images of fresh, delicious vegetables. For those who haven't had the pleasure, the Bowery is a very fun and vibrant neighborhood in downtown NYC, but it's not one in which you'd want to eat off the sidewalks. However, when we were naming the business, I happened to be reading a book about old New York, and learned that *bouwerie* is the Dutch word for "farm," and that's how the Bowery neighborhood got its name— from the original urban farms. It was the perfect symbol for the business and we liked that it was intriguing, possibly a bit controversial, and would get people's attention at the shelf. When so many of the names in the category were literal and functional (Organicgirl, Earthbound Farms), we took the opposite approach. In every decision that we made with Irving, we considered the layers of the brand experience. What would get people's attention in the produce aisle? A name and brand identity that didn't look like anything else. What would convince them to buy? The functional benefits they care about most (local, zero pesticides). What would get them talking about the brand at a dinner party and feeling good about their purchase? The brand's mission. It's all connected, and you can't successfully approach one element without considering the others. The emotional resonance of a brand is not something that can be invented from thin air. It has to be backed up by how a company actually behaves and the products that it sells. There needs to be connective tissue between what a brand says and does, and how it makes people feel.

———

In today's landscape, when consumers have more choice, knowledge, and power than ever before, you have to approach branding with integrity from the beginning. Before you even start to think about your logo, you need to figure out what you're aiming to do for people and how you want them to feel as a result. It's about creating an experience that solves real problems for people, and doing so in a way that makes them feel understood and uplifted. If the emotional territory you seek to own isn't grounded in the product experience itself, then it's just a nice story you're telling that dissolves the second someone scratches the surface. It's like clothing brands that feature plus-size models to create a feeling of inclusivity but then don't offer sizes above a 12 across their line (this is a real thing that happens, and it's frustratingly common).

Brand should never be a deception; it should be a delightful expression of a product's truth, and ultimately a positive force in people's lives. The brands that people love the most effortlessly combine the functional with the emotional. The product does what it's supposed to do, better than anyone else, and the brand makes you feel good about being part of its world. If you have one without the other, it's very difficult to maintain love and loyalty over time. But when you are able to achieve both, that's when people become obsessed.

> *Remember:* Consider each of your functional benefits, and how they can credibly ladder up to a unified emotional story. Identify all the things you will do to improve people's lives, and then figure out how people will feel as a result.

3

SENSE OF SELF

A FEW IPHONE ITERATIONS AGO, I GOT FRUSTRATED WITH Apple. I was having an insane amount of trouble getting my new phone to sync, in stark contrast to the days when it was so beautifully seamless to open any new Apple product and get it up and running. Pissed off and wanting to do something about it, I considered for the briefest of moments switching to Android. I looked into a few phones, asked my one Android-using friend for her thoughts (which were all very positive), and then very quickly came to the conclusion that even if the phones are cheaper and easier and had way better cameras, I just couldn't do it. I couldn't become a "green texter." Because, as the iPhone people know, when you text other iPhone users, it's through iMessage, and the texts show up in blue. But when you text with someone on any non-Apple device, the texts are green. At that moment, I resigned myself to my lifelong membership in the Apple cult. Apple may annoy me, its products may go downhill, its launches may disappoint, but an association with the Apple brand is too entwined with my own identity for me to walk away. Having an Apple laptop or an iPhone or AirPods signals something about what you care about (and your disposable income as well; let's not ignore that piece of the puzzle). Apple has done such a phenomenal job through the years of associating its brand with creativity and iconoclasm that people still feel cool and anti-establishment using its products even if everyone around you already has them. It's the ultimate example of a brand that has aligned itself with a set of values and become part of people's sense of self. It's Mac versus PC, and team Mac is for life.

BUILD YOUR BRAND AROUND THE CUSTOMER

In chapter 1, I talked about grounding your brand in the problem you're solving for people. Chapter 2 is about focusing on how you will make people feel. What each of these principles has in common is that the entire exercise of branding is less about you, and more about your customer. The most successful brands of today recognize that in order to create meaningful and lasting relationships, they need to find new and positive ways to tap into people's sense of self. They need to create brand identities that people want to identify with, from the beginning. Of course, leading brands have always tried to align themselves with their consumers. If you're a parent who cares about your baby's comfort, you buy Pampers. If you're someone who appreciates world-class engineering, you drive a BMW.

But these types of narratives are still inherently product focused. "Our product embodies x and y attributes, and by buying our product, you are stating that you care about these attributes." The difference with next generation businesses is that instead of inviting consumers to define themselves by choosing the brand, they align themselves with the values of the consumer. It's the difference between "buy this brand and make this statement about yourself" and "we understand you care about x, and we do too." It's about meeting consumers where they are, instead of trying to force them into the self-serving story that you want to tell. By flipping the equation on its head, branding becomes less about establishing your own identity, and more about creating a shared identity with your customers.

Nowhere is this shift more apparent than in the world of fashion. In so many ways, fashion is the perfect microcosm for the evolution of branding, because brand has always been the primary driver of decision making in this space. Yes, of course luxury brands have better construction, finer stitching, more-flattering cuts, but no one can deny that the strength of the brand plays a massive role in consumer choice and willingness to spend. You may make the argument that you're choosing a certain detergent because it washes your clothes better, but it's a lot harder to claim purely rational decision making when it comes to the clothes themselves. A free promotional tote is going to transport your wallet and keys just as effectively as a Chanel bag, but it's probably not going to make you feel the same way when you put it over your shoulder and walk out the door. Whether it's the maximalist designs of Gucci or the understated opulence of the Row, there are reasons that people are willing to spend thousands and thousands of dollars to align themselves with the images of these brands, and why there's a whole market around knockoffs. These labels carry a lot of weight, and certain luxury brands still do a great job of maintaining relevance, in spite of the fact that they represent a far more traditional, old-school approach to what a brand means.

However, an emerging movement is taking an approach that's the opposite of paying for the label. Instead of asking people to splurge in order to outwardly express something about themselves, these new brands are putting their values, not their logos, front and center. And those values tell a powerful story that's less about the company and more about the people who choose them. Contrary to a brand like Gucci, which creates a highly covetable but unattainable world that you can spend a lot of money to own a tiny piece of, emerging brands are inviting their consumers in with stories that intentionally stand counter to the traditional image-conscious approach. Everlane is the perfect embodiment of a modern fashion brand that's rooted in shared identity instead of image, and it does this by embracing transparency instead of mystery. Through its transparent practices, it has attracted a huge following of people who care about where their clothes come from and how they're made.

EVERLANE AND "RADICAL TRANSPARENCY"

In 2011, before Everlane even launched, it started to build an audience through its prelaunch referral program that offered tiered rewards for sharing with friends. Its message was simple but powerful. With an infographic released on Tumblr that quickly went viral, Everlane outlined the actual cost of producing a designer T-shirt and compared it to the typical fashion markup. It exposed the vast difference between the cost to produce an item (estimated at six dollars) versus what consumers are asked to pay (forty-five dollars). And, in contrast, it highlighted Everlane's fifteen-dollar price point for its simple, high-quality tee, the only item it would offer at launch. While the direct-to-consumer model was not unique to Everlane (Warby Parker, for example, was already in full swing), it was one of the first brands to outline in very plain terms the logic of removing middlemen and markups in order to deliver more value to their consumers. And this message resonated powerfully.

Q. Hold on. Isn't this approach the opposite of what you've been saying? By making it all about price, isn't Everlane eschewing emotional connection in favor of functional messaging, and commoditizing its offering?

While it may appear that way on the surface, Everlane was not selling a fifteen-dollar T-shirt on the virtue that it was just fifteen dollars. Its message was never about price itself; it was about fairness and honesty. Cheap T-shirts existed long before Everlane—you could go to the drugstore and buy a pack of tees in plastic wrap. But that's exactly what they felt like—cheap. And even if most consumers were aware of the outrageous markups in fashion, they either justified spending more for a high-end brand in the name of better quality or accepted how things were due to lack of appealing alternatives. What Everlane does so brilliantly is tell a story that puts it on the same side as its consumers. Instead of tearing down the idea of fashion and risk making people feel foolish for ever having cared about it in the first place, it offers people a new way to connect with a fashion brand. After all, fashion is fun, and the joy of shopping for clothes is not something that many people want to reject outright. People get pleasure from expressing their personal style through the clothes and shoes and bags that they buy, and Everlane gives them a smarter way to do so.

Starting with the infographic, Everlane's message to consumers is that it's not their fault they've been overpaying for clothing up until now. It's because of inefficiencies and deceptions in the system. By eliminating those inefficiencies and by embracing total or "radical transparency" as the brand calls it, Everlane can offer a T-shirt that's just as high quality but costs a whole lot less. So Everlane's consumer does not need to be a person who eschews quality to get a better deal. Rather, they're getting more value, and aligning themselves with a brand whose values match their own. Instead of people feeling like they're buying cheap stuff, or wishing they could afford luxury but settling for less, Everlane helps people feel smart. Once the math is broken down so simply, why would you pay the markup? Its consumers were able to join in a movement that was about bringing transparency to fashion, an industry in which it was sorely lacking. In Everlane's world, everyone knows exactly how much markup they're paying and why, which creates unity between the business and its customers.

Since launch, Everlane has seen incredible growth, of both its product line and the company. At every step, it has reimagined the relationship between a fashion brand and its consumers by bringing unprecedented openness to an industry that was typically shrouded in mystery and allure. This includes not just honesty around pricing, but an open dialogue about its manufacturing processes. For decades, the fashion supply chain has been a highly uncomfortable and troubling dilemma for many consumers, as stories will periodically surface about the terrible conditions in which much of our clothing gets made, before the public conversation moves on to the next topic. Does anyone else remember the huge stir BuzzFeed founder Jonah Peretti created in 2001 when he tried to get Nike iD to embroider *sweatshop* on his shoes, and then published his entire email exchange with customer service?

In the early 2000s, American Apparel tried to address this moral quandary with its "made in Los Angeles" and "no sweatshops" positioning. But after multiple exposés revealed the disgusting and abusive behavior of its founder and CEO, not to mention ad campaigns that claimed to be provocative but were quite disrespectful to women, the company could hardly be upheld as a paradigm of righteousness. And that's the key. A brand these days will likely run into trouble if it approaches one aspect of its business with good intentions but ignores ethics in another area. Consumers are trying to choose brands that align with their values through and through, because they want the brands they buy to support the identity they uphold for themselves. They are hungrier than ever for brands that they can feel good about buying, and that includes confidence that no dirty secrets will be uncovered.

Not everyone cares where their clothes are made, and the people who have no interest are probably not Everlane's consumers. But for those who do care, Everlane has built a brand that people can trust and align with, bringing what's usually behind the scenes to the fore-ground. In 2014, it hosted its first Transparent City Tour, in which it invited Instagram fashion influencers to visit its factory and dye house in Los Angeles. It also delayed the launch of denim, amid mounting demand, until it was able to find a factory that met its sustainability standards. The Vietnamese factory it ultimately identi-fied recycles 98 percent of the water used in denim manufacturing and turns the leftover sludge into bricks to construct affordable housing. In the months leading up to the denim release, Everlane shared photos and stories from the factory, creating an eager wait list of over forty thousand shoppers. On its e-commerce site, Everlane devotes an entire navigation link—precious digital real estate—to its factories so shoppers can explore exactly where they're shopping from.

Everlane also continues to transform the conversation around value, eschewing the more traditional discount-driven sales ap-proach for creative initiatives that provide more opportunity to build goodwill with its consumers. Instead of the standard retail post-Thanksgiving Black Friday sale, which draws criticism every year for encouraging rabid consumerism and spending around a holiday that's meant to be about gratitude, Everlane launched the Black Friday Fund, in which 35 percent of the day's revenue was put toward improving the lives of workers at its silk factories. The money went toward a new and improved recreation area that included a basketball court.

In 2015, Everlane launched its biannual "Choose What You Pay" event, through which it sells excess inventory at the end of each season. For each item, consumers are offered three prices, low, medium, and high, and get to decide how much it's worth to them. Everlane reveals exactly where the money goes, so, for example, the lowest price may cover product development and shipping to the warehouse, whereas a higher price will support overhead for Everlane's team. Compare this to reports of luxury and fast-fashion brands literally destroying their excess inventory in order to prevent it from flooding the market at discounted prices. With "Choose What You Pay," Everlane turns the whole idea of a sale on its head. Rather than slashing prices at the end of a season with no indication as to why something that once cost one hundred dollars is now seventy-five dollars, Everlane puts information and control in the hands of the consumer, and creates a new conversation around value.

Of course, these initiatives, while laudable, would not be enough on their own if the product did not deliver. Everlane has continued to evolve on the style front, too, coming a long way from T-shirts but staying true to its core approach. Its line of "modern basics" continues to expand while adhering to a classic, understated design ethos. The chic minimalism of its clothing is in line with the values of the company and its consumers: this is not a brand that shouts its name from the rooftops with flashy logos or colors. Once again, it taps into its consumers' sense of themselves as people who choose material and quality over image and trend. Nearly all of Everlane's new releases sell out and result in wait lists. It's not because the designs are particularly hot or "of the moment," like a street-wear drop or a splashy designer collaboration. Even as the brand has expanded into higher-end items at higher price points (e.g., handbags that cost a couple hundred dollars), it never feels excessive, and it continues to marry substance with style. The brand's pervasive feeling of quality and intentionality creates a point of pride in being an Everlane customer—you're buying into a set of principles about how clothes should be made and how much you should spend on them. It's a "badge brand" that stands for way more than just a badge.

While Everlane was one of the first, and certainly one of the most prominent, many brands now are seeing success by pulling back the curtain and creating a more candid exchange with their audiences. In an era in which anyone can tweet their feelings for all to see, businesses cannot afford to see brand as a wall that sits between them and the world, depicting a perfectly constructed image. Instead, brand needs to be seen as a tool for conversation, a way to expose your values so that consumers can make smarter, more informed and intentional choices.

BRANDING FOR INTENTION

The rise of the more thoughtful fashion brand signals a response to the larger consumer movement of conscious consumption. People are seeking brands that reflect their values, and brands are having to respond by making clear not only their purpose, but how they live up to it in action. Everlane's message of transparency wouldn't carry nearly the same weight if the company didn't have an entire section of its site devoted to its factories. It's no longer enough to talk the talk, not when consumers are being so much more thoughtful about what is worth owning in the first place.

Another newer fashion brand that has seen success by positioning itself against the old ways of the industry is Cuyana. Founders Karla Gallardo and Shilpa Shah set out to create a brand that inspires "intentional buying." The opposite of fast fashion, Cuyana uses the tagline "Fewer, Better Things." While the idea of a brand telling you to buy less may seem surprising or counterintuitive, this message has resonated deeply with people who are looking to fill their closets with items they are actually proud to own, rather than jumping on the next trend only to end up with drawers full of junk. Cuyana even has a Lean Closet program in which you can select an option at checkout to be sent a linen bag that you fill with items you no longer need. When you mail it in, you get 10 percent off your next purchase. The brand also partnered with Marie Kondo, the queen of decluttering, to launch a capsule collection of travel cases. Over a short period of time, Cuyana became a cult brand for women in the know, expanding from leather goods to a full line of apparel and raising $30 million from private equity in early 2019. In the era where *Marie Kondo'ing* has become a verb, combined with a new understanding of the terrible waste that fast fashion generates, Cuyana perfectly taps into the desire of people to be thoughtful and deliberate about what they buy and which brands they support. Brands now need to demonstrate they are worth caring about, by proving they care about the same things as their customers.

FEEL GOOD IN EVERY WAY

The beauty industry has been following a similar path as the fashion industry. Both of these categories have historically been defined by deliberate mystery. While certain skincare brands would herald a "hero ingredient" that claimed some kind of half-science, half-magic miracle breakthrough that gave women the power to stop time in its tracks, for the most part you had no idea what the hell was in this stuff. As with fashion, part of the appeal was the allure, the feeling that you were buying a secret formula that would quietly work its wonders overnight while you slept, and you'd wake up dewy and bright-eyed. You didn't need to understand it, not really—it just needed to work.

Much like transparency around manufacturing in fashion, the clean beauty movement has started a new conversation that puts the ingredient list front and center, once again putting more knowledge, and therefore power, in the hands of consumers. Brands like Beautycounter and Tata Harper, and retailers like Follain and Credo, are putting firm stakes in the ground that consumers should never have to sacrifice their own safety in the name of beauty. They highlight long lists of ingredients deemed to be dangerous and toxic, most of which are already banned in the EU, and vow to only make and sell products that don't include them. Beautycounter calls this list its

"Never List," which includes over 1,500 ingredients commonly found in cosmetics. The brand's founder, Gregg Renfrew, spends time lobbying for more government regulation of the beauty industry, and the business, which is a certified B Corp, partners with nonprofits such as Healthy Child Healthy World and the Environmental Working Group.

But here's the key, and here's what these new beauty brands understand and do well: safety on its own is not enough. Consumers are absolutely getting smarter about what goes into the products they put in their bodies and on their skin, and they are demanding more from the brands they choose. But they don't just want to feel good rationally: they want to feel good emotionally too. There's a reason that beauty is a multibillion-dollar industry. First, there's the fact that many believe in the power of these products: that great skincare products will make their skin look and feel better, that luxury makeup will go on smoother and last longer. Additionally, just like with fashion, this is a category that's been largely built through emotional drivers and aspirational imagery. So much of why people are willing to spend on these products is how the products make them feel, from the beautiful packaging to the boost in confidence. Not everyone wants to shop for a moisturizer in a health food store or make their own face mask at home. The clean beauty and skincare movement would not be seeing nearly the same traction if it ignored the fun, indulgent, luscious, luxurious, sexy side of beauty, nor if it ignored efficacy.

Transparency, performance, and the emotional lift all need to work together to create a brand with which people want to identify. Because people can feel good about what's in the products, they can feel smarter about buying them, more assured that they'll work, and ultimately better about themselves because they're choosing a form of self-care that's actually good for them instead of potentially doing harm to their bodies in the name of physical appearance. Instead of viewing beauty as a somewhat frivolous or even shameful indulgence, they can be proud that they're treating themselves with clean, wholesome products that work. And that pride can be perfectly expressed through a "shelfie," a posted photo of a bathroom shelf that includes a curated selection of beauty products that marry style and substance.

We worked with a leader in the clean skincare space, Ursa Major, to help the company evolve its brand and take credit for what makes it special. While many of our client relationships begin before launch, we also work to evolve existing brands. This doesn't mean you should set out to launch with one version of your brand and change it later: rebrands can be costly and time consuming. But change becomes necessary when the brand identity (logo, messaging, website, packaging) doesn't accurately reflect what the brand stands for, and the business isn't positioned for its next stage of growth. A similar dynamic was at play with the Airbnb example in chapter 1. When we work to evolve an existing brand, we are rarely reinventing its reason for being. Rather, these are typically brands that were ahead of their time, who helped pave the way for a whole new slew of successful businesses, but then find themselves being outshone or outpaced by newer entrants into the category. The new competition is rarely superior in terms of offering but has done a better job of storytelling, largely because they had the benefit of learning from and building upon the brands that came before them.

Launched in 2011, Ursa Major was one of the first of a new wave of premium, effective clean skincare brands. It had gained a lot of traction with its gender-neutral products, particularly its deodorant, which for many consumers is the "gateway" into cleaner products. However, since Ursa Major's launch, the clean skincare category had rapidly expanded, and "natural plus effective" was on its way to becoming the norm. Our work with Ursa Major was by no means a redo, as a lot of what was in place was working. Instead, we came on board to help sharpen the story by better articulating the values of the brand through language and design, as well as reimagining the e-commerce experience.

Ursa Major is a perfect example of branding that taps into people's sense of self, because the identity and values of the founders, the brand, and its consumers are nearly indistinguishable. Its founders Emily Doyle and Oliver Sweatman, a married couple, created the products they wanted for themselves, and in doing so have brought along many others who share their mind-set. Leaving behind high-powered careers in New York City, Oliver and Emily moved to Vermont to be closer to nature and to live a healthier, more integrated lifestyle. As Oliver tells it, "We left the city, a place we love, to pursue something totally different that was more in line with what we were looking for. That backstory of us moving to Vermont is important: that desire to follow your true north, which led us to the name 'Ursa Major' [the famous constellation that contains the North Star]." He describes the shared value between brand and consumer as "getting out there and enjoying the outdoors and the environment," saying, "This isn't just another personal care brand trying to get you to load up on as much product as possible. We want to give you awesome essentials, and inspire you to live your life."

After learning about the toxins that are present in so many personal care products, Oliver and Emily set out to create a line of sustainably made, natural products that didn't just work, but felt amazing to use. In many ways, the ethos of what they built stands in contrast to the rest of the industry. They wanted to be the opposite of brands whose packaging costs more than what's inside, and made a conscious decision to lower their margins in order to deliver more value. Gender neutral is also an important attribute of the brand and its products, and rare in a category that typically keeps men and women as separate as the beginning of a seventh-grade dance. Oliver and Emily spend years developing their formulations until they both love a product equally, and this ungendered approach to skincare contributes to the brand's straightforward, uncomplicated personality. Every choice they make purposefully rejects the excess and indulgence that often characterize skincare brands.

In describing their philosophy, Emily explains, "We have this very tight set of essentials that are head to toe. We've been around a while but we only have fifteen SKUs [stock-keeping units]. We never launch anything that we don't feel is truly amazing and an awesome product experience. It's not about giving people too many choices and making them feel they need it all." In other words, while every Ursa Major product is designed to deliver an amazing experience, this is not a brand that asks for hours and shelves devoted to self-care. Their story is not about embracing an involved beauty "routine." Instead, it's about washing your face and then getting out of your bathroom and into the world.

We worked closely with Oliver and Emily to articulate the brand's specific point of view, helping drive focus while preserving what was already working so well. Together, we landed on the idea of "low maintenance, high impact," the perfect description of both the products themselves and the people who embrace them. Ursa Major's target audience is people who value mindfulness and balance, and whose idea of luxury is unplugging, and enjoying nature rather than materialism. Oliver describes their "tribe" at length, painting a vivid picture of the "everyday explorer." He says, "It's not the traditional notion of exploration, someone wearing a Rolex on top of an iceberg. It's about inner and outer exploration, available to anyone at any given time. They're adventurous, they're actively solving for holistic wellness. They're proudly low maintenance." Ursa Major is not for everyone, and it doesn't care. By making clear its values—nature, mindfulness, vital living—it attracts the people who share those values and doesn't worry about the rest.

In fact, Emily and Oliver can speak at length not just about their target audience, but about who their products are not for. Emily says, "We talk about the more 'beauty involved' consumer: someone who spends a lot of time in the bathroom with rituals and steps and masks. That's a big part of their day and their self-care, and there's a lot of awesome things about that in terms of taking time for yourself. But that's not our customer."

We saw an opportunity in the notoriously crowded beauty category for Ursa Major to differentiate itself by carving out a space that's just as much about its consumers' identity as it is about its products. We positioned the brand as "premium, not precious," speaking directly to these consumers who pride themselves on seeking high-quality essentials over fads or gimmicks. This resulted in a down-to-earth but elevated approach that stands out against older natural brands that feel too earthy and homemade, and newer ones that feel overly pricey and excessive to Ursa Major's target.

Striking the right balance between "natural" and "premium" was an interesting challenge, as these two concepts generally don't live together. We did a photo shoot in Vermont that celebrated the brand and its audience's love of nature, knowing we may turn off people who would then see the brand as too outdoorsy and not traditionally luxurious enough. In fact, our team spent a lot of time questioning Oliver and Emily on their commitment to nature as part of the brand story; we were worried that a more urban-dwelling consumer may not relate, but they rightly held their ground. Oliver and I were looking back on these conversations, and he explained, "A lot of people have questioned it, but this is sacred ground for Ursa Major. We're never going to switch our Instagram feed to urban images, because we have a stake planted in the outdoor space. We always go back to our tribe and our insight. The way we think about the outdoors simply amounts to quality time outside—it can be on the West Side Highway [in New York City] running down by the river, or a weekend escape, or a two-week hike."

He sees Ursa Major as a breath of fresh air, the antidote to big-city grooming, which also ties into the emotional territory that we identified as "invigorating." And the brand doesn't try to do it all: "Our goal is not to be the go-to for everybody. We don't need ten million customers to be an awesome business. We need a fewer number of really committed folks who share our values. As long as we're appealing to those people, we don't care about everyone else."

Ursa Major's supreme clarity on its tribe is not a value judgment about one set of attitudes versus another. We worked on another skincare brand, Then I Met You, whose philosophy and target audience is quite different from Ursa Major's, leading to its own unique space in the category. Founded by Charlotte Cho, the successful entrepreneur behind the wildly popular Korean beauty site Soko Glam, Then I Met You's positioning is rooted in the Korean concept of jeong, which is all about taking the time to form deeper, more meaningful connections. Then I Met you embraces the "double cleanse," a staple of the ten-step Korean beauty routine in which you wash your face first with an oil cleanser followed by a water-based cleanser. The brand celebrates spending time on yourself, away from distraction, and putting in extra effort to yield meaningful results. As it states on the site, "At Then I Met You, we believe now—in the age of distraction—it's time to go deeper. By adding a little extra effort in the right places, we believe you can spark meaningful, transformative moments in your life, and create lasting bonds with the people, places and things that matter most." The person who adopts the double cleanse is a different person than the one who wants a brisk, refreshing face wash to then be on their way. And it's not just about their skincare habits. Those who fall in love with Ursa Major or Then I Met You do so because they see themselves in the brand: its approach matches their approach to personal care and healthy living.

YOUR PRODUCT BETTER LIVE UP

What Ursa Major and Then I Met You have in common is that their products very much deliver on their philosophies. The risk of seeking a connection that's rooted in shared values is that brands have to live up to their promise, or they're going to get called out. The second a brand makes a claim to stand for something, there's an army of commenters waiting to jump on the slightest whiff of hypocrisy or inconsistency. And this is a good thing, as it forces accountability and prevents brands from paying lip service to ideals that they don't actually embody. When Allbirds first launched, it was very careful to talk about its sustainability mission as a journey, knowing it would be a few more years of innovation until every part of every shoe could be made from renewable materials.

In fact, one of our clients redid its entire product in order to better live up to the values of the brand and its consumers. We first started working with dating app Hinge in 2015. At the time, the dating app craze was in full swing. Tinder launched in 2012, and completely transformed the world of digital dating with its swipe functionality. Before Tinder, sites like Match and OkCupid required their users to fill out and sort through profiles, reading up on a potential date's interests and passions and attempts to be witty before connecting. Tinder blew that all up, putting forward the bold perspective that people only care about the pictures anyway, and taking advantage of mobile technology to create an experience where all you had to do is swipe right or left on a person's photo to indicate whether you're interested or not. Hinge launched shortly after Tinder with similar functionality, the main difference being that you signed up through Facebook so you would be connected with friends of friends. The idea was that this vetted community more closely mirrored whom you'd want to meet in real life, such as at a friend's party or wedding. Instead of connecting with people based on proximity, you could meet people who were one step away from the people you already knew, and who were therefore part of your extended circle.

As these things sometimes go, Match, OkCupid, Tinder, and Hinge are now all owned by Match Group. But at the time of launch, Tinder and Hinge were competitors. We started working with Hinge with the goal of evolving the brand, corresponding with the launch of a new set of features. Hinge was planning to expand its functionality to connect people based on not just shared acquaintances but also interests. So if you absolutely loved independent film, or cooking, you would have the opportunity to meet people who also love those things. We created a strategy that was about forming real connections by discovering the unexpected things you have in common with people, and we were nearly through building the evolved brand identity, which included a new logo in which the middle bar of the *H* could be swapped out with icons that represented shared interests. Picture two parallel lines connected by a taco, a camera, a book, etc. in order to form the *H* of Hinge. We felt it was simple and clever, directly conveying the new feature that Hinge saw as the future of its differentiation. We left for Christmas vacation feeling pretty good about ourselves, and then got back in January to . . . nothing. No word from the Hinge team on final feedback or next steps. And let me tell you, when you're in client services, no news is rarely good news. Though, in this case, we were not expecting what came next.

As it turned out, Hinge had spent early January at a team off-site, going over the new brand strategy and identity. Its founder, Justin McLeod, along with the rest of the team, had come to the conclusion that while they were on board with the vision of the new brand, their product didn't live up. How could they be the brand for people who wanted to find more genuine connections when its main functionality was still swiping on pictures of people's faces? It didn't feel right, and the changes they were planning felt incremental instead of substantive. In early 2016, Justin made the bold decision to reimagine and rebuild Hinge from scratch, which meant also starting over on brand. Their team got to work on a new product vision—they were going to get rid of swiping, and instead orient the experience around full profiles rather than just photos. Users would only be shown a certain number of potential connections a day to discourage endless, mindless scrolling, and would indicate interest in another person by commenting on part of their profile, encouraging more meaningful interactions. As the Hinge team worked through product, we went back and revised our brand strategy, specifically targeting people who were seeking relationships, and positioning Hinge as a more human dating experience for those who want something real. Hinge set out to make it clear that they were for a certain kind of person, someone who is looking for a substantive experience. No judgment on the people looking for one-night stands, but Hinge was not for them. From there, we created a new logo in which the *H* and the *i* connect to signify the start of a relationship journey, as well as form a subtle nod to the very human, natural greeting of "hi." The new Hinge launched summer of 2016, revealing itself as "the Relationship App."

Match Group acquired a majority stake of Hinge in spring 2018 and completed its acquisition the following year. It may seem odd to think of Hinge and Tinder under one roof, but once they became brethren instead of competitors, each was able to home in even more clearly on whom it's for and what it stands for. Tinder's first major brand campaign, created by famed advertising agency Wieden+Kennedy, proclaimed that "Single is a terrible thing to waste." The campaign joyfully and unapologetically embraces the fun of being single, speaking directly to young people who aren't necessarily looking to settle down. While typical dating brand communication is all about finding that special someone, Tinder's campaign acknowledged its audience and their priorities in a new, refreshing way by highlighting the good parts of being single, and the values of freedom and independence. Meanwhile, we created a campaign for Hinge around the tagline "Designed to be Deleted," which states that Hinge exists to help you meet someone, so you can quit Hinge (at least for a bit). The campaign makes it clear that Hinge is for people who are seeking fulfilling connections, and aren't just looking to play around on dating apps with no end in sight. For the campaign, we created a fuzzy character, Hingie, who symbolizes the Hinge app. Every time a couple gets together, Hingie dies again and again in a bunch of different, creative ways; for example, one ad shows a couple in the background snuggling in a tent, while in the foreground Hingie roasts in the campfire (no actual Hingies were harmed in the making of this campaign). The message of the campaign is that "Hinge wants you to find love. Even if it kills us." Some people will see themselves in the Tinder campaign: you're a person looking to make the most of your single years. Others will align with Hinge: you're a person looking to make a meaningful and lasting connection, and get off the dating apps. Each campaign signals to its specific community that the brand is for them.

BELONGING TO THE CLUB

It's particularly helpful for dating apps to broadcast so clearly who they're for, because it means that when people are on the app, they're more likely to meet like-minded people who share their attitudes toward dating and are looking for the same thing. But even outside the realm of dating, branding is at its most powerful when it speaks to people's sense of self. It creates a community, not just between brand and consumer, but among everyone who loves the brand. When people choose a brand these days, they're making a statement about their values, and in doing so, they're connecting to others who share those values. When I see someone wearing an Aviator Nation sweatshirt, my favorite Venice Beach–based sweatshirt brand, I immediately feel a sense of kinship with them, like we're part of the same club. I have to stop myself from giving them a knowing nod, as if we're already buddies, because that would be weird. Subaru WRX owners actually do wave to each other (like people on boats!). When a brand successfully taps into people's identities, it creates a movement that's about more than the brand. The brand starts to function as a sort of connective tissue, a real-world hashtag that signals a shared set of values across different groups of people: I see you wearing the same sweatshirt as me, and I see something of myself in you. When people choose which brands to love, they're choosing which part of themselves they want to convey to the world.

Remember: It's not just about how you want your brand to be seen. It's about connecting your brand to how people see themselves.

4

CREATING CONNECTION

STARTING IN 2015, SEEMINGLY OVERNIGHT, A STRANGE PHE-
nomenon had overtaken every single one of our clients' offices. Every fridge in every startup in New York City, including ours, was
suddenly filled with LaCroix. As far as I know, this wasn't a coordi-
nated takeover. I don't think all of the office managers got on a conference call and decided to order this old flavored seltzer brand en
masse, or that LaCroix sales teams sneaked into buildings under
cover of darkness and restocked all the kitchens. Yet there it was,
everywhere. And this surge in popularity wasn't exclusive to New
York startups. People started publishing lists ranking the flavors. Co-
workers everywhere could be found having heated debates about
whether coconut was delicious or disgusting, or both! Here was a
decades-old brand that had suddenly sparked a mass obsession.

Plenty of articles have been written about the causes of its new-found popularity—everything from changing health trends and diets like Whole30, to influential bloggers, to its flavor strategy—and we don't need to go down that rabbit hole. What's interesting to me about the LaCroix phenomenon is what it exposes about the role that brands play in creating collective identity. In the early 2000s, there was a Diet Coke on every desk of my ad agency, and cans of soda filled the conference rooms. Today, as many people have come to reject fake sweeteners and unknown ingredients, I've never seen a Diet Coke within the walls of my office. It's simply not part of the shared identity of our team; it doesn't fit in. To be seen with one would almost feel like being caught with a cigarette, as extreme as that sounds (though I will admit I still love to drink Diet Coke at home). The ubiquity of a brand among a set of people is more than just a shared set of tastes; it's a shared set of values. The communal choice of one brand versus another unifies a group of people around what they care about. It builds a sense of community.

WHAT COMMUNITY REALLY MEANS

Effective branding is all about creating connections. By tapping into consumers' sense of their own identity, brands build a connection with their audiences. People feel an affinity toward brands they love that extends beyond their relationship with the products. It's not just about what functionality a product provides; it's the way the brand makes them feel about themselves. But it doesn't stop there. The brands that achieve true cultlike status create a sense of connection not just with their consumers, but among them too. A camaraderie forms among people who love the brand, even if they never actually interact with each other. If a brand speaks to their identity and their values, then it follows that people would feel connected to others who share those values. That's how businesses with a clear sense of purpose are able to build a community in ways that other similar businesses can't.

Q: Does this mean I should focus my marketing efforts on getting people to like my Facebook page?

Many brands today talk about a desire to build community, but it isn't always clear what that means. When we meet with a new business that says community is important to them, we urge them to think about how they envision this community coming to life. Just like *authenticity*, *community* has become such a buzzword that every brand thinks they need it, even if they don't know how to define it. The rise of social media is a key driver in this new focus on community. In the era of social media, it's possible, in ways that were never possible before, for brands to have actual "conversations" with their consumers, and this creates both pressure and opportunity to connect in new ways. Theoretically, those consumers could also be interacting with each other, but the reality is that in most cases consumers are not spending time talking to each other on a brand's Facebook page. And should that even be the goal? When is the last time you had a conversation with a stranger on a brand's Facebook page? It's a great sign of consumer enthusiasm when a social media post generates a lot of activity, but likes and comments on Facebook or Instagram should not be equated with "community," and only represent a narrow, literal application of the term. In fact, the brands that aim solely to build a community in the comments section are missing the point. The brands with the strongest communities are not necessarily those with the most-active Facebook pages. People do not need to be digitally interacting with each other, or even physically interacting, to feel they are a part of something together. When brands are able to create unity around shared values from the beginning, community forms.

The brands that have successfully built community are the brands that people mutually obsess over, and this shared obsession creates a bond among strangers that is felt even if it can't be seen. A sense of community then further fuels people's affinity for the brand, creating a virtuous cycle that strengthens loyalty among the group. These brands harness the power of collective experience to establish a following, even in categories where you might be surprised to find a rabid fan base. It's one thing for community to form around a brand like CrossFit, where people are actually interacting regularly with a set of like-minded others. (Plus, who doesn't love to talk, and talk, and talk some more about their workout?) But there are brands in other categories that have succeeded in creating a shared connection that far exceeds expectations. Sweetgreen, the chain of salad-based restaurants, is a perfect example of a brand that built an unlikely community and created a phenomenon.

COLLECTIVE CONNECTIONS

When Sweetgreen launched in 2007, salad was not a new idea. You could, and still can, build your own salad at pretty much any deli in any city in America. Chopt, a salad chain that on the surface is pretty similar in concept to Sweetgreen, had been around since 2001. If anything, the workday lunch salad has become a bit of a cultural joke, with memes like "women laughing alone with salad" (a collection of stock photos depicting exactly that, assembled by blogger Edith Zimmerman) and the phrase *sad desk salad* (what it sounds like) taking hold. Sweetgreen has not only escaped this derision, but has created a world that people are proud to be part of. If any other salad is a "sad desk salad," Sweetgreen is an occasion within the workday. A disproportionate amount of our team's Slack channel activity centers on who's going to Sweetgreen to pick up everyone else's orders, and I'm sure we're not alone. It's hard to think of another lunch chain that inspires such enthusiasm, and it's because from the beginning, Sweetgreen stood for something greater.

Sweetgreen started as a single location, opened in the Georgetown neighborhood of Washington, DC, by three recent Georgetown University grads, Jonathan Neman, Nathaniel Ru, and Nicolas Jammet. From the start, the founders were dedicated to building a brand that was about much more than lettuce. Functionally, they set out to solve a fairly obvious problem: a lack of healthy, delicious, and convenient food. It's a problem that many a brand, from fast-casual restaurants to packaged goods, has set out to tackle. But Sweetgreen took an approach that elevated the brand beyond the functional benefits of the food. Yes, the ingredients are fresh, the recipes are inventive, the dressings are delicious; without all that, Sweetgreen would not have gotten off the ground. However, the brand doesn't stop there. The founders set out to change people's relationship to their food, with the mission to "inspire healthier communities." Sweetgreen's definition of community is wide-ranging: it includes the farms from which the company sources its ingredients, the neighborhoods where it opens stores, the company's employees, and of course the customers, with the brand at the center creating a positive ecosystem. Its mission is infused throughout the entire experience, defining the in-store experience, the digital experience, and all of the brand's activity.

The irony with Sweetgreen is that most chains are generally viewed as the enemy of community, coming into neighborhoods and replacing local businesses. I am not here to argue that point, or whether cities would be worse or better off without Sweetgreen. Certainly one could make the case that Sweetgreen's customer base represents a homogeneity of class and experience. But what can't be debated is that Sweetgreen has smartly made deliberate choices to avoid that generic chain feeling of being in a Subway or McDonald's, or even Starbucks, where you could be anywhere in the country or the world. When Sweetgreen opens new locations, it seeks out distinct spaces and works to preserve the natural structure of the building, embodying a neighborhood instead of invading it. As it says on Sweetgreen's site, "Our guests don't go to a Sweetgreen, they go to *their* Sweetgreen." Within the spaces, Sweetgreen displays the works of local artists, further driving home a sense of specificity and localness.

Sweetgreen also behaves differently from most other multilocation restaurants in its approach to food, focusing not just on flavor or health but on how its food connects to a set of shared values. It has created a transparent supply chain, working with local farms that share Sweetgreen's ethos of sustainability and animal welfare. In every Sweetgreen location, the restaurant's food sources are listed, creating a clear link between the brand's customers and where their food comes from. This creates a new feeling of connection between consumers and the farmers who supply the food they eat, something that's sorely missing in the modern industrial farming era. While you might expect to see a list of sources at a high-end farm-to-table restaurant, in fact, in their everyday lives, people are offered very little knowledge of where and how their food is grown, and whether it aligns with their values. By listing its sources, Sweetgreen invites its customers into its mission every time they buy a salad, strengthening the feeling of community.

The brand also partnered with renowned chef Dan Barber, famous for his purpose-driven approach to food and farming innovation. In 2015, they worked to create the Blue Hill salad, which incorporated overlooked food scraps like kale stems. And in 2018, Sweetgreen's menu featured a proprietary squash breed, the Robin's Koginut, grown with seeds from Barber's new company, Row 7. Barber and Sweetgreen share the mission to reduce food waste, and Sweetgreen consistently designs its menus around what farmers are growing, versus requesting specific crops. Its ingredients are delivered each day, and its food is made fresh on location, in an open kitchen for all to see.

It also made the subtle but purposeful decision for one employee to build a customer's entire salad, versus setting up food preparation like an assembly line. While this may not seem like a big deal, it gives the consumer a sense of personal touch when their food is created, rather than just moving through an automated process. Each of these behaviors ladders up to a feeling of shared commitment: to our planet, our health, and our fellow humans. The sense that people are all connected—that our choices in where we eat affect the planet, that we should be aware of the people growing and preparing our food—creates a palpable sense of community, with the brand at its core.

Sweetgreen's focus on community has driven the brand to expand into territories one wouldn't have thought possible for a chain of salad restaurants. For example, in 2011 it launched a musical festival called Sweetlife at the seventeen-thousand-seat Merriweather Post Pavilion in Maryland. Music had been part of the brand's DNA from the beginning. The founders had set up a DJ booth to attract foot traffic outside their Dupont Circle location in the early days, and they held a couple of live music events with pretty major acts in the store's parking lot, which drove sales and, more important, buzz. Launching Sweetlife felt like a natural progression, but the scale of the event was impressive. Headlined by the Strokes, the first year also included talent such as Girl Talk and Theophilus London, and the event was sponsored by like-minded brands such as Applegate Farms and Honest Tea. Sweetgreen was even able to persuade the venue's food services company to serve healthier options than typical concert fare. The festival continued annually for a few years and attracted big-name acts like the Yeah Yeah Yeahs, Lana Del Rey, and Kendrick Lamar, who even collaborated on a limited-run menu item, Beets

Don't Kale My Vibe. Eventually, the founders decided it made more sense to return to a smaller scale, more intimate events strategy, but Sweetlife's run provides an excellent example of the brand's dedication to community building. It's hard to picture another restaurant chain throwing an event of this size without it feeling lamely corporate. Sweetgreen had enough credibility with both artists and its audience to pull off a high-caliber music festival, and that's because of its genuine commitment, built into its DNA from the beginning, to bringing people together. It was a bold move that set the brand apart from its category and bolstered its position as far more than just a place to get lunch.

It's not just splashy music festivals: Sweetgreen's values are present in its everyday behaviors. The brand is known for its generous customer service policy, responding quickly to complaints and typically offering a full credit toward the next purchase, no questions asked. Its loyalty program also offers an exclusive customer service email for people who reach the highest level (Black), which requires a $2,500 annual spend. While that may seem like a lot, with salads around thirteen dollars a pop, there are enough people with a daily Sweetgreen habit who qualify. Customers who have reached Black status also get to throw an event for ten friends at any Sweetgreen location, in addition to receiving free swag. As Sweetgreen explains on its site, "At this point, you're essentially family to us. We know you by name + salad and may have even met your parents." Plenty of places have loyalty programs, but Sweetgreen's creative approach to rewards (access to invite-only events, the ten-person salad party, a portion of your purchase donated to Sweetgreen's charity) serves to reaffirm a sense of camaraderie and joint purpose. You don't just get free salads; you get to take part in the Sweetgreen world.

Of course, Sweetgreen's mission of "inspiring healthier communities" could run the risk of feeling disingenuous if all the company did was sell expensive salads to well-off professionals. But its commitment is proven further through its social good initiatives, beginning with Sweetgreen in Schools, a program that launched in 2010 to provide curriculum and workshops on health and sustainability to students across the Northeast. In 2019, Sweetgreen partnered with nationwide nonprofit FoodCorps to support its Reimagining School Cafeterias program. The program's goal is to connect kids with healthier food options by offering them better access along with the ability to interact with and have a say in what they eat. Sweetgreen's social programs align perfectly with its overall mission, so rather than feeling like an afterthought, they're a natural extension of the brand. It all ties together: the brand's approach to ethical food production, linked with its commitment to teaching young people about better food choices. It doesn't feel like Sweetgreen is simply paying lip service to the idea of giving back; instead, the notion of community grows even deeper. Just like a brand's purpose, "community" can't be created from thin air, or conjured by a clever approach to social media. The most successful communities develop organically when a brand adheres to a clear set of values, and a natural connection forms among those who are not only buying the products, but believing in the ethos of the brand.

GOING DEEPER FOR THE CAUSE

For decades, brand marketers have been shown some version of a stat that [insert large percentage] of people are more likely to buy a product if the company gives back in some way or is associated with a good cause. "Cause marketing" has been around since the 1970s, and the form it typically takes is that some percentage of your purchase gets donated to a philanthropic cause. Cause marketing's peak season is October, Breast Cancer Awareness Month, when countless brands sell a pink version of their product and donate a portion of proceeds to breast cancer research. If you read the small print, these donations are often capped at a specific amount, but even with a cap, it's hard to criticize a business for trying to give back.

Q: So if I want to build a brand that gives back, should I just pick a cause I care about and donate to it?

It's certainly better for a corporation to donate any amount of money to a charitable organization than none at all. However, from a brand-building or even cause-building perspective, the "*x* percent of proceeds" approach can feel a bit shallow. Many times the chosen nonprofit has very little connection to the product itself, and the brand does little to educate consumers about the cause or inspire them to get further involved. A cynical view would be that that these brands are doing the bare minimum: minimum amount donated, minimum effort. These programs often don't feel that thoughtful, and can sometimes feel tacked on, rather than inherent to the brand's purpose and story. As such, they do little to build community.

Modern brands are now finding more-creative ways to align themselves with causes that feel far more integrated and purposeful, such as Sweetgreen's partnership with FoodCorps. Toms Shoes is undoubtedly one of the originators of this new wave of giving back, in which social responsibility is not an add-on to the brand's story but is built into the brand identity itself. Founded in 2006 by Blake Mycoskie, Toms created the now ubiquitous "one-for-one" model: for every pair of shoes that Toms sells, it provides a free pair of shoes to children in developing countries. The brilliance of the Toms model is its simplicity, and therefore its tangibility. Toms could have taken the approach of donating a portion of profits to organizations fighting poverty, but it would not have had the same power in generating a movement. With the "X percent of proceeds" approach, there are too many layers of abstraction: consumers have no idea what a company's proceeds are, let alone what 1 percent or 10 percent translates to. Nor do they have a clear sense of where that money ends up and the potential effect it might have. With the Toms approach, a consumer can actually visualize their impact: they buy a pair of shoes, and someone who needs a pair of shoes gets one too. The original Toms shoe design was incredibly simple, too, and therefore unmistakable. The shoe's unique silhouette quickly became iconic—people loved it or hated it as a style statement, but everyone knew it was the "one-for-one" shoe.

When you put on a pair of Toms, you weren't just wearing any old pair of generic slip-ons. You were making a statement about your values, and connecting to a group of people who all believed in this new, altruistic brand that was unlike anything that had come before it. You were wearing your beliefs on your sleeve, or, in this case, your feet. Toms grew incredibly quickly, and a lot of its growth came from press and word of mouth. People were excited to learn about and talk about this new kind of business model that opened possibilities of what companies could achieve for the world. Toms is not a non-profit, but it does represent a new era of "conscious capitalism." Its business model is inherently tied to its social mission, and conceiving of one without the other is impossible. There is no Toms without "one-for-one." That's another way to think about incorporating social good into a brand's story: if it's a tiny appendage that can easily be lopped off with no effect on the overall brand identity, you haven't gone deep enough.

Toms was able to rapidly build community because people felt connected to the brand's mission, and therefore to others who were wearing the shoes and also believed in the mission, and to the children across the world who received a new pair of shoes because of a Toms purchase. That powerful sense of connection created a movement that took off. People could directly understand their impact through the product itself; they could look at their feet and feel good about their contribution. Even the Toms logo, a simple all-caps font within two horizontal blue stripes, feels like a flag. The brand is inviting you to be part of a nation of people who believe in doing things differently, for the good of the world. After Toms' early success, it's not surprising that other brands adopted the one-for-one model. When Warby Parker first launched, a big part of its story was its "buy a pair, give a pair" program. This includes training people to administer eye exams and sell affordable glasses, as well as giving vision care and glasses to students in need. The Warby Parker website details the impact a pair of glasses has, the countries it has reached, and pictures of people who have benefited from the program. Again, this is impact people can see and believe in, rather than some vague promise to donate money.

Bombas is another rapidly growing brand whose story is very much rooted in a one-for-one model. Just like Toms, the Bombas brand was born from a built-in desire to have an impact, versus introducing impact as a marketing tool. Its founders, David Heath and Randy Goldberg, were struck when they learned that socks were the number one item requested at homeless shelters. Inspired by the success of Toms and other companies like it, they decided to create a business in which for every pair of socks purchased, a pair would be donated to a homeless shelter. Smartly recognizing that the mission itself would not be enough to drive obsession, they went on a journey to construct the perfect pair of socks, and were able to identify several key areas in which sock material and construction could be improved to deliver a significantly better product. They also created a special pair of socks for donation, designed to withstand multiple wears with fewer washings. Here was a category that hadn't seen innovation in who knows how long, and it certainly hadn't seen an inspiring brand. With a better product and a compelling story, the founders initially raised money for their 2013 launch through a very effective crowdfunding campaign on Indiegogo, and ultimately received backing from *Shark Tank*'s Daymond John, who cites Bombas as one of his most successful investments to date.

For most people, socks are an afterthought, certainly not an item to pay a premium for. But Bombas proved that people were willing to spend more on a better constructed sock from a brand they believe in (at about eleven to sixteen dollars a pair, its socks are not cheap). What's more, people are excited to talk about Bombas and spread the word; it's the first sock brand that people brag about wearing. When someone discovers Bombas, they can't wait to tell others about it. That kind of growth via word of mouth happens because Bombas is the whole package. The business was started from a genuine desire to create a positive impact on the world, but the founders didn't just throw a new brand name on a cheap pair of socks and hang their whole story on the social mission. They put a great deal of effort into designing substantively more-comfortable socks. This allows community to form across multiple angles: there are the people who are inspired by giving back, and also those who love to spread the word about this amazingly comfortable new sock brand they found. Because the donation program has been an inherent part of Bombas from day one, it doesn't feel heavy-handed, it's just an inextricable part of the story. The brand identity is rooted in the mission, but not in a way that feels preachy or self-righteous. Instead, it invites everyone to get on board.

The name Bombas comes from the Latin word for bumblebee, creatures that work together to create a better environment for everyone, but if you didn't know that, it's also a fun-sounding, energetic, and memorable word. Building on the name, the logo is a bee with a crown, and many socks feature a hive-like pattern. "Bee better," the brand's motto, is stitched inside each pair, a statement that speaks to giving back but also to personal achievement and the innovation of the product itself. The overall effect is a combination of playful and inspiring, a brand that does serious work while not taking itself too seriously. It all works together: the product, the mission, and the feeling the brand gives, creating an optimistic and colorful world that people are proud to be part of. Community grows through collective enthusiasm, for the products themselves and the good the company does.

Consumers are not just aware of the values of these brands, they're inspired by them, and this bolsters a feeling of taking part in a collective movement. Consumers are "voting with their dollars," putting their money behind the brands they believe in, and joining a team of others who are doing the same. However, while connection to a social mission may feel like a shortcut to building community, it's not as easy as writing a check and calling it a day. Successful brands of today embody their commitment to social good through and through: in how they make their products, in the programs they develop, and in creating innovative ways to effect change, like the one-for-one model.

This deeper approach to a social mission is demonstrated in the evolution from "cause marketing" to "corporate social responsibility" (CSR), in which a company's social consciousness is built into its business model. Companies who actively engage in CSR find ways to make a positive impact (and avoid a negative one) in their everyday practices. Rather than a short-lived marketing campaign, it's an inherent part of how they operate, and core to their brand. As with all successful, long-term brand building, it's not a layer that sits on top, but an idea embedded within the organization.

WE'RE ALL IN THIS TOGETHER

Enthusiasm for a joint cause is a powerful community builder, but that doesn't mean that a brand has to have a social mission in order to create a collective movement. What matters is that people have something to rally behind, to get excited about. This could be anything that generates passion. Passion is powerful within an individual, and unstoppable when it's shared. When a brand creates a movement, it's because of shared passion. There are certain categories that lend themselves more easily to this kind of group frenzy. I mentioned fitness before; music is another. There are few forces more powerful than music for bringing people together. But that doesn't mean that any brand related to music is an automatic home run (just ask much of the music industry). The most successful brands in the space recognize that music becomes even more meaningful when its listeners feel linked to each other. That's the unmatched energy of a concert: it's the camaraderie among fans who aren't strangers, because they love the same band. Spotify has done an amazing job tapping into this strength to build the leading music streaming service worldwide. From the start, Spotify was never just about a more convenient way to access music. Instead, it finds new and interesting ways to connect its users to each other and feel like part of something bigger.

Spotify's approach to community building is inherent within the product itself. Much of its experience is oriented around user-generated playlists, which have become the modern mixtape, but instead of just passed among friends and crushes, they're shared with everyone on Spotify. If you love '90s hip-hop, for example, you can follow playlists created by Spotify, or those created by other users from around the world. You can follow your friends to see what they're listening to, and broadcast what you're listening to, including on other platforms like Facebook. This creates a connection among Spotify users, along with a more human and personal way to discover new music that's not just generated by an algorithm. Fans around the world can share their taste and knowledge as part of a broad community of music lovers.

Spotify's active and engaged community is one of its most valuable assets, and the service very cleverly celebrates this unique advantage in its advertising, developed in-house by its creative team. Starting in 2016, Spotify began running a global end-of-year outdoor campaign that highlights its user data in surprising and hilarious ways. Billboards feature headlines such as "To the 1,235 guys who loved the 'Girls' Night' playlist this year, we love you," and even hyper-local lines such as "Dear person in the Theater District who listened to the Hamilton Soundtrack 5,376 times this year, can you get us tickets?" Each year since, Spotify has updated the campaign with new data, revealing the quirky and fun behaviors on its platform. In increasingly divided times, the Spotify campaign uses humor to celebrate individual points of view ("Eat vegan brisket with the person who made a playlist called 'Leftist Elitist Snowflake BBQ'") while also drawing connections among people ("Dear 3,749 people who streamed 'It's the End of the World as We Know It' the day of the Brexit vote, hang in there"). Ultimately, the campaign reveals what people have in common: the many ways in which we use music to celebrate good times and weather the bad, and the offbeat preferences that we're not alone in having.

The message is that we're all human, music is part of what makes us human, and therefore we can all belong to the Spotify family. You can chuckle at someone else's unusual playlist while reflecting on your own musical tastes and your beliefs in general. The campaign creates a sense of warmth and connection among total strangers, as you feel compassion for the "person in LA who listened to the 'Forever Alone' playlist for 4 hours on Valentine's Day." You don't need to know who they are, or see their Facebook profile—we've all been that person. We are less alone with Spotify connecting us. In recognizing the humanity of its member base, Spotify creates an intimacy among its users that makes them feel closer to each other and the brand. It feels more like a club than a global tech platform.

Q: I get how you can build a community around music. But what if my business is in a category that doesn't naturally bring people together?

Of course, Spotify has an advantage, existing in a category that so naturally lends itself to emotional resonance. But every business is targeting people who share a set of needs or preferences, or who are at a specific stage in their lives. There are many ways to forge deeper connections among those people, which then strengthens their connections to the brand. Some brands have robust and active reviews sections, in which people share not just opinions on the product, but tips and suggestions. Others highlight individual member stories on their Instagram accounts, celebrating the real people who are using their products every day. The more intimate and tightly knit a brand's community feels, the greater the brand's reach can be. It's the difference between a community and a crowd. Within a community, each person matters—you're part of the group and you're contributing to the whole. You aren't just an anonymous individual among the faceless masses. You belong.

SPEAKING THE SAME LANGUAGE

Brands build strong communities by ensuring that everyone who takes part in the brand feels like an insider. There are many ways to generate this feeling of belonging. It can come from a shared sense of purpose: you care about the same values and causes. A shared uniform: you are proud to be wearing the same brand as other people like you. And shared vocabulary. A brand's verbal identity, how it speaks, is a valuable community-building tool. Through its choice of language, a brand indicates who it's for and, just as important, who it's not for. For example, a brand that wants to indicate that it's for people with a certain level of expertise may use terminology that isn't common knowledge among the general population. A cookware brand that's targeting cooking enthusiasts may talk about blanching or sous vide without providing definitions. The same can be true for sports brands, gaming, any category in which a set of people prides themselves on having deeper-than-average knowledge.

Brands need to navigate these decisions carefully, because most businesses do not want to turn people away by seeming unapproachable or overly exclusive. But there's also danger that comes from aiming to reach everyone. If you're trying to target experts, for example, and your language is overly simplified, you run the risk of seeming like a brand for novices, and the quality of your product can be called into question. Is this espresso maker really the best if it's for people who don't know what a *cortado* is? Category enthusiasts do not want to feel talked down to; they don't want to be part of a community in which terms they know well need to be explained.

The same philosophy applies for choice of expressions and use of slang. Warning label: brands need to be extremely careful in their use of slang. More often than not, a brand that tries to dabble in "how the kids are talking these days" comes across as trying way too hard. It's like hearing your dad use slang (i.e., excruciating). As with most things, if in doubt as to whether you can pull it off, you probably can't. But for some brands, a specific conversational approach is inherent to their identity. They wholeheartedly embrace a set of words and phrases that speak to a certain audience, and don't worry about turning off the rest. Just like among a friend group, this creates a common bond, a sense of shared understanding and insider status. You get it, or you don't, and if you don't, then it's not for you anyway. Perhaps the best example of a brand that leans in very hard to a specific way of speaking is the Skimm.

Founded in 2012 by roommates Carly Zakin and Danielle Weisberg, the Skimm started as a daily email newsletter and has evolved into a suite of products and services that include a podcast, a book, an app, and other resources that make it "easier for you to live smarter." The newsletter is the heart of the brand, with seven million subscribers as of late 2018. It provides a morning rundown of the important news of the day, written in a casual, conversational tone that is unlike any other news source. The Skimm starts each news story with a funny headline in its signature style, which either prompts what's coming in a tongue-in-cheek way ("Who's searching 'the best lawyers in the UK' on Yelp . . . Julian Assange" or "What has less of a conception of privacy than your parents . . . Facebook") or plays the role of the reader, prompting more information. Unlike brands that deliberately target experts, the Skimm unapologetically writes for people who are not news or politics obsessed. It removes the shame of not knowing the answer, starting new paragraphs with phrases like "I feel like I've heard about this before" followed by "you probably have. This has to do with the Iran nuclear deal." Or "I'm gonna need a quick history lesson," which leads into "the Gaza Strip used to be controlled by Egypt . . ." Each newsletter provides a self-contained briefing; its readers can stay up to speed on current events without possessing a wealth of knowledge about what came before. It's written in the tone of two friends chatting, but finds a succinct way to deliver valuable information.

The Skimm's unique tonality has made the brand the subject of some criticism and derision. Journalists have accused the Skimm of dumbing things down or treating serious subjects too casually. But clearly the Skimm has done an incredible job of connecting with its audience, motivating a massive number of people to engage with the news and politics, and even getting people to vote with its nonpartisan "No Excuses" campaign. The Skimm has also succeeded in mobilizing its users to spread the word about the brand through its Skimm'bassadors program, which rewards members for sharing the

Skimm, offering swag, access to events, exclusive content and networking opportunities, and birthday shout-outs in the newsletter. Zakin and Weisberg have spoken publicly about their comfort in creating a voice that's not for everyone. They are crystal clear on who their brand is and how it behaves, with an internal brand guidebook that outlines the tastes and habits of "the Skimm girl," which continue to evolve over time as trends change. And the Skimm's loyal audience continues to grow, which flies in the face of accusations that the brand is somehow condescending. The people who get it feel like they're part of a community, all the more because not everyone needs to get it.

Brands build successful communities when they create a powerful feeling of inclusion. This does not require purposely leaving people out, but it does require a willingness to put a stake in the ground about who you're for and what you stand for. When Patagonia began refusing to sell its fleece vests to corporations that don't prioritize the planet, it may have disappointed some Wall Street bros, but it augmented the love of its environmentally conscious audience, who felt even more connected to its values, and therefore more loyal to the brand. When people know what a brand stands for, and they agree with it, that creates an intimate bond. Communities form not around a logo, or a clever social media strategy, but a shared set of passions or ideals. Once again, there is value in building a brand from day one that stands for more than just a product story. While there may be an initial burst of enthusiasm when something launches that works really well or has a cool new feature, that enthusiasm is unlikely to sustain itself over time. When brands invite people to become part of a community, its consumers are much less likely to move on to the next shiny thing, because they would lose a collective connection that's become part of their identity.

Remember: Community is not defined by your number of Instagram followers. Instead, real community forms when you find ways to connect your consumers through a shared set of values.

5

STRENGTH IN FOCUS

RECENTLY I HAD TO BUY AN AIR CONDITIONER, AND THE experience was so unpleasant, it made me wonder if I should just embrace the heat. There were so many brands to weed through, and even within those brands, a million choices of features and functionality, with no clear way to determine what actually mattered. What was worth paying more for? Do I care more about quiet or efficiency? After extensive research on Wirecutter, reading reviews, and asking around for recommendations, I finally made my decision, only now there was the hassle of getting it delivered up the stairs in my non-elevator building and installed. The entire ordeal made me realize just how spoiled I've become by the direct-to-consumer modern brands. How lovely it is to shop on a website that offers just one model. How reassuring to know you're paying the best price without shopping around, and that customer service is both reachable and on your side. And how much more fun it is to choose a brand whose entire experience has been singularly designed with your needs in mind. There's a lightness and freedom that comes from not having to choose, because the work has been done for you. Who wants to spend their time comparing features and reading reviews? I'd much rather just be told the answer.

THE POWER OF FOCUS

In chapter 3, I talked about how brands should think less about their own identity and more about how they can tap into the identity of their audience. In chapter 4, I looked at how in order to build community among a set of people, a brand can't try to be all things to all people. Both of these principles require speaking directly to a specific mind-set, which means making choices, sometimes even tough choices, that drive focus. The successful brands of today aren't afraid to home in on a clear point of view, rather than attempting to cover all the bases.

Brands that are looking to grow ultimately need to reach a very wide audience, and that audience isn't going to look identical to the people who first fell in love with them. While there are plenty of "niche brands" these days going after small slices of small markets, powered by the razor-sharp targeting capabilities of Instagram and Facebook, many new brands are still aiming for massive scale. But even if the goal is to build a billion-dollar business, without that first set of people who get behind a brand and become its loyal following, a brand will never have the chance to attract the rest. Those initial brand champions fall in love because they know exactly what a brand stands for, and what it stands for speaks directly to them.

With the seismic shifts in how culture gets consumed, the fact that any new brands are able to reach mass scale is actually a bit unbelievable, seeing as it's less and less the case that people are all watching the same shows or shopping at the same stores. I remember, somewhere around the year 2000, reading a magazine article about TiVo that was the reason I decided to pursue a career in advertising. For those of you who were born in the year 2000 (or, gulp, after), TiVo was one of the first digital video recorders (DVRs) that enabled people to record shows from cable, watch them later, and fast-forward the commercials. And *cable* was . . . oh, you know what, don't even worry about it. The point is, the idea that you could watch a show anytime you wanted, without ads, instead of when it was "on TV," was monumental. In the article, it talked about a future without TV advertising, and purported that we would have a difficult time explaining to our grandchildren that we once all bought the same brand of detergent. The article predicted the demise of a unified consumer culture, which had been largely created by TV advertising. At the time, I started thinking about the fact that people did all buy the same brand of detergent (at least for now), and the role of marketing in a product's ability to tap into universal human needs. That summer, I got an internship at an ad agency to better understand how brands were able to communicate in ways that reached so many different people, and what that said about what connects us all. Fast-forward to now, and even the idea of a DVR feels positively antiquated in a world where many people don't have cable. But amid the fall of monoculture and the rise of e-commerce, the significance of brands that we all know, and more important love, hasn't gone away. It's just that brands today need to find a different path to growth, and it starts with focus.

There's a reason that most of the successful new consumer brands launch with a very limited offering. Instead of coming out of the gate with forty different styles, each in ten different colors, many of these brands launch with just one or two products. On the surface, this approach may seem like it gives consumers less control, but it's actually about removing false distinctions that waste people's time and make their lives harder. This stands in contrast to the days of traditional retail, where brands would try to launch as many individual items as possible in order to dominate the shelf. That's why you might see twenty different types of the same brand of toothpaste at the drugstore and subsequently spend a half hour deciding if you care more about tartar control, whitening, tartar control plus whitening, extra-fresh breath, or the ability to chew through cardboard. Now, it's about recognizing what people want, and serving it up simply and succinctly. These brands are doing consumers a favor by curating the choice for them, and consumers reward them in return. The brand builds loyalty and then is able to gradually introduce more products over time, in a controlled, digestible way.

SIMPLICITY IS A GIFT

More than anyone could have imagined at the start of this insane century, we are in an era of information overload, choice overload, decision overload, shows-to-binge-watch overload. There are thousands of ways to be entertained, millions of places to shop. But instead of this fragmentation leading to a different detergent brand for every zip code, successful new brands have realized that reduction of choice is a benefit in itself. By simplifying their offerings, brands are able to focus more on an emotional overarching narrative than minute product differences. At Red Antler, we worked on a project (that never ended up launching) with a traditional accessories company who was hoping to build a direct-to-consumer brand. We debated with them for months trying to get them to limit the number of styles and colors at launch. Their merchandising team could not wrap their heads around why we would want to go to market by offering people fewer options, because you would never approach a buyer in a department store that way. But one of the beauties of the direct-to-consumer model is that by offering less, at least to start, you can get right to the heart of the brand story instead of spending time helping people navigate through endless product variations.

Many of the direct-to-consumer new companies' success stories have taken this more focused approach with their product strategy, which in turn has afforded them the ability to build a beloved brand. By offering less, these brands can stand for more. Away, the luggage brand valued at $1.4 billion as of 2019, launched with just one product in 2016. Away was founded by two former Warby Parker employees, Steph Korey and Jen Rubio. (Korey temporarily stepped down as CEO in late 2019 amid negative press, but was then reinstated.) When the brand first launched, its only product was a hard-shell carry-on suitcase. It was priced affordably at $225 with a lifetime guarantee, and offered in just four colors. Instead of spending time explaining the differences between its various models and helping consumers decide which one is right for them, Away focused on its singular offering to enable a launch that was all about people's love of travel. Travel, not luggage, provides a rich and resonant narrative canvas, and the brand tapped into this emotional territory from the start. Toward the end of 2015, when Korey and Rubio realized their product would not be ready for the holidays, they launched a preorder strategy that enabled them to tell a focused story about the brand. They interviewed interesting, influential people from the creative community and created a hardcover book called *The Places We Return To*. Everyone who preordered a suitcase received a copy of the book, which ended up selling out. This approach set the tone for the brand from the very beginning, that its purpose was to connect people over a shared passion for travel, with the suitcase as a means to an end.

Launching with one style can also lead to faster impact, because the product is instantly recognizable as a symbol for the brand. People can spot the Away suitcase, or the Allbirds Wool Runner, and it says something about those carrying or wearing it. The Away carry-on's iconic look immediately became a symbol for a travel-oriented lifestyle. Even when Away launched additional styles in Fall 2016, it did so in a way that avoided traditional decision fatigue. In addition to the original carry-on, it added the Bigger Carry-On, the Medium, and the Large, names that made the differences between each style immediately clear. On its website, a comparison tool makes the choice even simpler by highlighting not just the suitcase dimensions but how many outfits each fits and the length of trip and flight that it's best for. This provided a far more human and approachable way to shop—who can really picture what 21.7 inches looks like? But you do know how many outfits you want to pack. Compare this to a brand like Tumi, which offers the Tegra-Lite Max International Expandable Carry-On, the Très Leger International Carry-On, the Arcadia International Expandable Carry-On, the Sutter International Dual Access 4 Wheeled Carry-On, and about a billion more. By the time you're done wading through the choices, you've missed your flight. Away's method gets you excited about where you're heading, instead of stuck on a website clicking into product descriptions to try to glean the minute differences.

As Away has grown, it has continued to reinforce its positioning as a travel brand. Its tactics have expanded, but its focus remains. It launched a quarterly travel magazine called *Here*, sold online and in its showrooms (and given to everyone who purchases a suitcase). In 2017, it took over a Paris hotel during fashion week to create Chez Away, a pop-up hotel with in-house manicurists and tattoo artists, as well as workshops and events hosted with like-minded brands. In summer of 2018, it launched a pop-up experience called Terminal A in NYC's SoHo neighborhood. The space, which was inspired by airports but far more stylish and without any TSA-induced headaches, sold Away goods along with other travel-related items. When Away began to open permanent retail locations in 2018, it curated other "travel essentials" to sell alongside its own products, positioning its stores as the place to "build your travel uniform."

Q: Don't all of these marketing activities and new products detract from the brand's initial focus?

Creating a brand with focus doesn't mean that companies need to only sell one product forever. Since launch, Away has expanded into accessories like Dopp kits and packing cubes, along with a line of aluminum luggage, and will no doubt continue to grow its offering. But it's doing so from the position of already establishing itself as the "travel lifestyle" brand, which then gives it permission to enter all kinds of travel-related spaces, from products to experiences. Instead of trying to gain mindshare by selling as many products in as many variations as possible out of the gate, it launched on the basis of an idea, and has since been steadily increasing the ways in which it delivers on that idea for its consumers. A laser-focused product strategy actually enables greater breadth of vision, because it's not the features of one suitcase versus another, it's about travel as a whole.

THE NEW LOYALTY

Away successfully recognized an opportunity in the fact that few people felt deep loyalty or love toward their luggage brand. Before Away, there wasn't an obvious brand that met the needs of the modern traveler, in the way it was priced, sold, and positioned. The era of browsing for a $1,000 suitcase at a department store was over, at least for most people, but nothing aspirational had risen in its place. Even the idea of a department store feels outdated in the digital age, and of course traditional retail is feeling the pain year after year. Many new brands are seeing success by scooping up the people who still need to buy a suitcase, or a mattress, or a set of dishes, but would rather do pretty much anything other than spend their Saturday at Bloomingdale's or Bed Bath & Beyond (and why should they, when everything they could ever possibly need can be bought on their phone?). These new brands launch with a clear, focused value proposition, and transform what used to be an annoying chore into a no-brainer.

We helped launch Snowe, a brand that, like Away, recognized that as consumers rejected the behaviors of the past, they needed somewhere new to turn. Snowe was founded by Rachel Cohen and Andrés Modak, a married couple who couldn't believe how difficult it was to shop for products for their home. On one end you had Ikea; on the other, overpriced department store brands. As Andrés describes it, "The problems we set out to solve were ones we encountered in our own experience as a couple setting up our home together. The price-value equation was broken. You see a lot of disposable quality and mediocre design, brands that are all about quantity over quality. But then the luxury brands were outside our reach. No one was making it accessible in a way that was compelling."

Finding no brand that offered fairly priced but high-quality home goods that matched their taste and vibe, they built Snowe, a direct-to-consumer home essentials company. Think plates, glassware, sheets, towels: all of those basic things that every house needs, the stuff that people used to register for when they got married. The insight behind Snowe is that most people aren't picking out china patterns, investing in a "good set" of dishes (for when the queen comes to dinner!), or stocking their closets with guest towels. Most people are not waiting until marriage to "build a household together." As a culture, our whole approach to living has gotten so much more casual and streamlined, and people need one set of dishes that's just as well suited for cereal in front of the TV as it is for a dinner party. Again, it's about removing the mental and physical clutter created by unnecessary choice.

Q: How does offering multiple product categories at once speak to focus? Shouldn't Snowe have initially stuck to one category, like just dishware or just towels?

Focus doesn't always look the same. While for a business like Away, it made sense to launch with just one suitcase, that's not true for every product category, especially when you think about sets of things that naturally go together and would be far easier to buy together, rather than visiting individual websites for every purchase. Snowe was able to offer a better experience for its consumers by providing them with one destination for all the non-furniture items that fill their homes. Through its guided, singular shopping experience, Snowe simplifies choice. Andrés explains, "Previously, you would sift through fifty open tabs online, shopping the big retailers and trying to decide what to purchase. You would walk into Bed Bath & Beyond and feel like the walls were closing in on you." Once Rachel and Andrés saw their opportunity, they had to ignore the naysayers who told them they were crazy to go after multiple categories simultaneously, expressing doubt as to how they would execute better than the companies that focused on just one product. They looked at what categories made sense to buy together, thinking about how to make it easy for a customer who has likely not made these decisions before, who is graduating beyond Ikea and cares about taste and quality, as well as price. "To cut through the noise, we needed to simplify and streamline the process, and become a one-stop shop."

It made perfect sense for Snowe to offer solutions across the home and create greater lifetime value with its customers, but the brand is still extremely deliberate in its assortment. The site navigation is organized around the main activities of the home: Sleep, Bathe, Eat, Drink. Choices exist only where necessary, and in those cases, the differences are made clear for consumers.

For example, when the Snowe team launched pillows in soft, medium, and firm, they included photos of a potted plant on each of the pillows to demonstrate the amount of give. Snowe also doesn't offer a million different patterns and colors. It's less about embracing a specific look and more about a feel that everyone can appreciate—the lightweight but durable dinner plate, the drinking glass that feels great in your hands, the perfectly soft towel. As Andrés explains their product philosophy, "We wanted to go after the true essentials—the core pieces that you can, in a very simple way, build on over time, layering and combining."

Snowe does extensive research and testing around the key elements that drive product decisions, to guide each product's differentiation. Innovations include titanium coating on a glass so you can bang it on the table or chuck it in the dishwasher, and air-weave towels that are much softer and dry faster. Andrés explains, "We didn't launch linen for two and a half years, even though it was gaining ground in the US, because we didn't want to launch for the sake of launch. Instead we spent over a year perfecting our product, developing a process that whips the linen with hurricane-force winds until it's so soft, you can't even believe it. If it's just about 'good enough,' there's enough of that out there. We're seeing the commoditization of so many products, especially with Amazon. But we're going after a more considered consumer. These are people who believe that 'less is more,' and who want to invest in pieces that last longer."

Our brand strategy for Snowe was "ground your life in beauty," expressing the idea that the items you use each day should provide a thoughtful and meaningful base layer for your life. We launched the site with the headline "Start with Snowe, see what happens." This communicated the brand's philosophy, that a dinner plate is not an end in itself; it's the means to create an experience around food. It should quietly and perfectly do its job, each day, for years on end. In other words, you shouldn't have to think about it too hard. The brand's focus makes shopping easy for Snowe's consumers, and not just in terms of convenience (though of course there's that too).

It's easy to sign on for Snowe because its value proposition is so clear. You can trust its quality, and stock your whole house without worrying about which coffee mugs to buy or even where to buy them. The entire feeling of the brand combines thoughtful, highly considered design with a relaxed, easy, modern lifestyle. It's not about obsessing over glassware; it's about investing in well-made pieces so you can enjoy them every day, however you choose to. As Andrés says, "It's about eating and sharing meals. A glass of wine at the end of day. We want to build an aura of intrigue and interest for the moments that live beyond the products. The products act as an anchor that makes experiences more enjoyable."

The website's photography embraces messy real moments like dishes in a sink instead of a perfectly curated, totally unrealistic view of life. All through the site, little surprises show up when you roll over certain product images: M&M's in a bowl, half-eaten macarons on a plate, a goldfish in a wineglass, an ice cream sundae in a martini glass. Amid its chic, minimalist designs, the brand conveys that it doesn't take itself too seriously, because neither do its consumers. This is where you can buy the products that will last a lifetime, but it's attainable and unpretentious. Among the brand principles is "Keep it simple," but, as Andrés explains, "The details matter so much. That's the paradox. We keep things simple, but we sweat the details to the nth degree. Every little detail matters that much more, because the customer that's more considered wants a much better experience. We never overdo it, and we never launch things that we aren't over the moon about."

Snowe provides an antidote to the fact that we have too many choices at our disposal today, which has frankly become exhausting. As a result, people don't want to have to work too hard. If they have to spend too much time researching, or go out of their way to buy something, or wait weeks for it to arrive, or (gasp) pay for shipping, they're going to opt out. That creates space for brands to swoop in with a focused message, a clear path to decision making, and a generous return policy, and it becomes so much easier to fall in love with them, because there's so much less standing in the way. By getting all of that distraction and friction out of the way, brands can skip straight to the fun part, inhabiting a world that's less about logistics and more about lifestyle. When choice is more of a burden than a gift, the brands that don't force people to think too much win.

SOME THINGS TO A LOT OF PEOPLE

While it may seem like giving people as many options as possible is the generous thing to do, it nearly always benefits the brand more than it does the consumer. It's actually more work up front for the brand to zero in on a vision from day one, forcing a hierarchy of benefits instead of trying to say everything at once. To drive obsession, brands need to be comfortable leaving some sets of consumers and opportunities behind. I've seen too many investors pitch decks that are trying to capture every potential path to growth under the sun ("right now we're about pets, but this idea can quickly morph into targeting seniors"). But to bring up everyone's favorite maybe-not-so-friendly giant, Amazon started out just selling books (the paper kind!), and it did so very well.

It's not easy for a new brand to edit its offering before it launches. There's risk involved, because from a business perspective, you may be missing out on potential revenue streams. Take the example of Away: there are likely some consumers who will only ever buy a soft suitcase. By launching with a hard case, Away left those people out of its set of potential customers. But as its one style quickly became iconic, its business became profitable in a very short amount of time, and it built credibility as a travel brand, which gives it permission to ultimately expand far wider than luggage. If Away had tried to launch with ten different suitcases, travel accessories, toiletries, and a hotel, the idea that it would have been able to do all of those things equally well with thoughtfulness, service, and storytelling is difficult to imagine. Greater focus gives the brand more room to control the narrative of what it stands for, which is necessary when a brand is aiming to transform and own a category. Focus can also help wake people up to new behaviors, because a brand can go deep on one message out of the gate, instead of spreading itself too thin too fast.

Drybar is a great example of a brand that saw amazing success by removing choice from the beginning. The idea of a salon blowout was nothing new—there are hair salons in pretty much every neighborhood in America, and all of them, it's safe to assume, have hair dryers. But Drybar founder Alli Webb identified a consumer need for an affordable blowout outside the context of the full suite of salon services. A trained hairstylist turned stay-at-home mom, she started in 2008 with a business called Straight-at-Home, in which she offered in-home blowouts that she advertised on mom-targeted blogs. When the demand became too much for her to meet alone, she launched a brick-and-mortar location in the Brentwood neighborhood of Los Angeles in 2010, under the Drybar brand.

From the start, Drybar made its offering crystal clear with the tagline "No Cuts. No Color. Just Blowouts!" This singular focus created a new occasion for a set of women who weren't previously thinking about frequent "just because" blowout appointments. The offering is so simple and straightforward, and priced reasonably enough, that it makes it easy to just say yes. Whereas going to the salon could feel like a chore or a special occasion, Drybar felt like a place to just pop in or meet friends. You can be in and out in less than an hour, and leave with the unique confidence that comes from feeling good about your hair. In fact, Webb has stated that Drybar is not selling blowouts, it's selling the happiness and confidence of a great hair day. By focusing on a specific need, Drybar gives people permission to indulge when they may not have otherwise done so. There's no decision fatigue, no effort, just fun.

Drybar has done an incredible job of brand building, creating a delightful experience through and through. Whereas the salon industry, especially in the mid- and lower-market, feels fragmented and unpredictable, Drybar is all about consistency, from the quality of its services to the feel of its locations. Leaning into the "bar" concept, it created a menu of cocktail-themed blowout styles, from the Manhattan ("sleek and smooth") to the Southern Comfort (big hair, lots of volume, naturally). This takes the burden away from the consumer to explain or even know what they want; they can just choose from the book, complete with pictures. The instantly recognizable brand palette of yellow and gray dominates the spaces, which are all equally bright, clean, and cheerful. Classically beloved "chick flicks" play on TV screens, and women are offered free wine or champagne and cookies. There are also small touches that make a huge difference in the quality of experience, like phone chargers at every station, an overlooked pain point in most salons. Even the bathrooms are charmingly decorated, with vintage black-and-white photographs on the walls and pops of bright yellow.

Drybar also creates a consistent experience among its stylists by investing in their education instead of requiring them to pay for their own training as most salons do. All of this put together means that stepping into a Drybar location is a guaranteed pleasure, and you know you will walk out looking and feeling wonderful. Today, Drybar has over one hundred locations across the US. In 2013, it launched its own line of styling products, including hairdryers in its signature yellow, which are sold at Nordstrom, Sephora, and Drybar locations. Perhaps the greatest evidence of its success is the number of similar businesses that have launched in its wake, both direct copycat competitors in the blowout space, as well as other single-service establishments in adjacent categories, like eyebrow shaping.

Webb has reported getting pressure from investors to expand beyond blowouts, but says she would rather continue to do one thing well and preserve the authenticity of the brand. And Drybar's focus goes a long way in communicating the quality of the brand's offering. Even if you didn't know about its investment in its stylists' training, you can more easily believe that the brand delivers an incredible blowout if that's all its stylists do. It's the difference between a high-end restaurant that offers a few carefully curated menu selections, versus the forty-page manual you're handed at the Cheesecake Factory. Focus can help convey an attention to detail, an ethos of quality over quantity. It can also help people understand that a brand is for them, by virtue of the fact that it's not trying to be for everyone. But again, that requires the bravery of leaving some people (and their wallets) behind.

Miko Branch, founder of Miss Jessie's, a multimillion-dollar line of haircare products, credits her success to an early conviction to own a clear segment of the market. In the '90s, she and her sister Titi opened a salon in the Bed-Stuy area of Brooklyn. Miko had just had a baby, and as she explained to me, "As a single parent, I was adamant to be fully present in my son's life while I worked in my shared home salon business with my sister Titi. I had to embrace my natural texture after my son splashed around at bath time on the fourth floor of our brownstone. I could no longer maintain straight relaxed hair, with no time to restyle my frizzy hair back to straight while running down to the second floor on the parlor level to service our clients." However, this practical necessity led to a transformative discovery, when, as Miko told me, a "small handful of clients showed more interest in my natural hair texture versus my relaxed and straight style."

Miko realized there was no market supporting African American women who wanted to wear their hair natural, so she set out to create one. Her salon stopped offering relaxing services, which was risky in terms of revenue, but as she explains it, "There was nothing to lose. We were less nervous about the change of salon services to our customers, and more concerned that we would not be able to pay the mortgage." She developed a new technique for styling curly hair, and curly-haired women of all races and ethnicities from all over the city started traveling to the salon. When Miko and Titi couldn't find products to support their styling services, they created their own from their kitchen table, and Miss Jessie's was born with its signature offering, Curly Pudding. In 2010, Miss Jessie's entered 250 Target locations, and today it's sold in Target, Walmart, and other nation-wide chains. Over the years as the business has grown, the natural hair movement has grown as well, with Branch as an established leader in the space.

The Branch sisters' decision to become natural and curly hair salon experts proved to be larger than anything they could have imagined, and their product innovation took it to another level. Their techniques and product line made them pioneers. And Miko has stuck to her focus over time: "No retailer, private equity firm, angel investor, or competitor has ever been able to compromise the equity built in our brand. Being our authentic selves, making the best decisions based on our values, has served us well both personally and professionally."

MADE FOR EACH OTHER

A singular vision helps build trust with consumers: they feel understood instead of upsold. Miss Jessie's well-defined offering, starting with the elimination of relaxation services in Miko Branch's salon, let women with natural hair know that their needs were not an afterthought, but the driving force of the brand story. Fueled by technology, brands have taken this idea further in the form of advanced customization. Instead of a wall of products overwhelming you with minute differences that all sound kinda important, these new brands are taking focus to the next level by offering one product that's tailored to a consumer's exact needs.

Customization is the ultimate expression of focus, because instead of continuing to expand a product line to meet every person's needs, one offering can be adapted to fit the different needs of each individual. Sticking with haircare, a quick browse of the traditional brands in the shampoo aisle will reveal separate products for reducing frizz, repairing damage, increasing volume, thickening (which is different than volume, please don't confuse the two), nourishing, protecting color, treating dandruff, and smoothing—this is all *from one* brand. But what happens if you have color to protect and frizz to fight? What then? (Asking for a friend.)

I spoke earlier in the chapter about the false distinctions that serve a brand more than its consumers. One solution is to remove choices and make it simple. The other antidote is to learn exactly what people want, and make it for them. We worked with a brand called Prose that set out to disrupt haircare with an unprecedented level of customization. Prose's cofounders, CEO Arnaud Plas and VP of product Paul Michaux, met at L'Oréal, and saw an opportunity to build a new kind of haircare business that more effectively answered the needs of the consumer and addressed common pain points.

Starting with shampoo, conditioner, and a hair mask, every Prose product is made to order. As Arnaud explains it, "Prose was started to challenge the beauty industry by pioneering a new approach to hair care, one that truly offers truly customized products and counters mass production. We saw the industry creating hair care products by hyper-segmenting consumers' needs into categories such as damaged, frizzy, 'ethnic,' etc. This outdated approach is overly simplified and does not allow for individuals to truly address all of their hair needs and goals, leaving customers with an army of products that are ineffective." Prose developed a proprietary algorithm that uses 135 different factors to determine a blend of ingredients, and creates a formula for customers that is 100 percent unique to each individual. It looks at everything that could have an impact on an individual's hair—specific environmental aggressors, scalp condition, stress level, diet, and more.

Instead of a traditional shopping experience, consumers answer a set of questions that results in their unique formulation. They can also indicate preferences like vegan or fragrance-free. Every answer impacts the formulation, which means consumers no longer have to choose which benefit matters most to them, but instead receive a product that's tailor-made for their hair, their behaviors, and their values and goals. While it may seem counterintuitive to ask consumers to spend time filling out a questionnaire in this era of convenience and speed, Paul shares the logic behind the consultation: "We understand that 25 questions might be a lot, but we've noticed that consumers who are passionate about finding best-in-class products will take the time. Consumers in this era are more willing to purchase from brands who align with their personal values and truly address their needs and desires. Amazon has set a precedent when it comes to fast, online shopping, but on the flip side, consumers are now looking for more immersive, conversational shopping experiences." Prose's platform offers customers a new type of experience, and its high conversions are proof that it's working. With customer feedback it can introduce new ingredients, advance its algorithm, and build meaningful relationships with its customers.

Our strategic idea for Prose was "hair like no other," a double meaning that speaks to the fact that every person's hair is unique to them, but also that Prose offers you the hair of your dreams. We created a brand identity that celebrates the precision of Prose's customization. The labels on each bottle are custom printed with the consumer's name and zip code, the expert stylist behind the formulation, and the main factors that influenced the formula. There's an almost scientific feel to the design, highlighting both the quality of the product and the ethos of the brand. For Prose, customization is not just a gimmick or a marketing tactic; it's the driving force behind the business model, allowing the brand to deliver greater value across the board to its consumers.

Arnaud describes three main areas of opportunity driven by customization, beginning with efficiency: targeting and addressing specific needs and desires leads to more effective products. The second opportunity is inclusivity; while other brands target a specific ethnic group or gender, Prose makes products for the individual. The third opportunity is sustainable production. Products are made to order, only after a customer's order has been processed, which leads to dramatically less waste than the rest of the industry.

From inclusivity to sustainability, the Prose brand celebrates a new kind of luxury that's a departure from the sleek glossy packaging of high-end salon brands. Instead, it's the luxury of a product that fits your values and has been created for you and you alone—your name is printed on the bottle, lest anyone forget or your boyfriend try to steal your shampoo. Further driving home the thoughtful and precise nature of the brand, the Prose site highlights its use of only the highest quality ingredients, followed by a list of ingredients it will never use. It separates its naturally derived ingredients from the man-made ones, with asterisks next to the ingredients that the company is working toward removing. This level of transparency provides reassurance that its custom formulas will be both safe and effective, removing all worry or decision making from the equation. No more experimentation or piling on multiple products to get a desired effect. Prose takes care of your hair for you, diligently, responsibly, and luxuriously. As Paul says, "We want a customer to feel like they are completely taken care of and truly special when they interact with, order, and use Prose. That is what modern luxury is to us."

Prose takes a new approach to a category that was historically defined by endless new product launches, each promising the next miracle solution while forcing consumers to decipher claims and choose among minutiae. Prose offers one solution that's made for the consumer. If one's hair changes as they age, or they move to a humid climate, or they start coloring, they don't need to do the research to find a new set of products; Prose can adapt with them. While a bespoke solution may sound more complicated on the surface, it's simpler for the consumer. Guesswork is removed from the equation: they're in the hands of a professional.

The appeal of customization has also taken hold in the health and wellness space, another category traditionally racked by an overabundance of choice. Care/of offers vitamins and protein powders that, like Prose, are formulated for each individual consumer. Few categories are more confusing than the vitamin and supplement space; not only are there thousands of different brands and products, there's also a ton of conflicting information, not to mention that it can be very hard to even know if something is "working." Without an immediate feedback loop, for many people fish oil may as well be snake oil, and the choice of which vitamins to take can be so intimidating and overwhelming that people opt out altogether.

A brand like Care/of has the opportunity to bring more people into the category through its guided, focused approach. Once again, choice is removed from the equation, and consumers only need to be an expert on themselves. No research or deliberation is required; simply answer a set of questions on your basic information, your goals, your lifestyle, and your values, and you're given a recommendation with which vitamins to take and why. Care/of may recommend rhodiola if you're feeling burnt out, or vitamin D if you live above a certain latitude. It's all spelled out clearly and succinctly, in a brand experience that's upbeat, modern, and unintimidating. The packaging is clean and direct, with the consumer's name printed on Care/of's custom vitamin packs, along with helpful health tips for the day. Even if you choose to shop à la carte, Care/of makes it easy by clearly outlining the purpose of each vitamin, supplement, and herb. Compare this experience to attempting to browse the aisles at a Vitamin Shoppe or GNC, or wade through dusty bags of herbal remedies in the back of a health food store, and you can see why Goldman Sachs invested in Care/of at a valuation of $156 million in 2018.

CHOOSE WHAT MATTERS

More and more brands are embracing the idea that consumers would prefer to have the decisions made for them, in contrast to the notion that people value choice above all else. This can happen through the removal of options, customization, or consultation, which works for brands like ThirdLove, which leads its consumers to the exact right bra based on a quiz to help them find their perfect fit. While its bras aren't custom made, ThirdLove gives custom recommendations, removing the stress that many women feel when it comes to determining their bra size and shopping for bras in general. ThirdLove also introduced half-cup sizes, and uses real women's measurements to create its products, offering seventy-eight different bra sizes.

Q: I thought you said brands were offering fewer choices in order to better serve their consumers? How does offering seventy-eight sizes translate into focus?

While the breadth of ThirdLove's assortment may seem contradictory to the notion of focus, brands that offer more options in the name of inclusivity, whether it's size or skin tone, aren't falling into the same trap as the brands that offer endless product variations for no good reason. After all, one individual consumer is rarely shopping among multiple sizes, but instead is seeking the size that's just right for them. And ThirdLove helps them find it. Prior to brands like ThirdLove, the only option for women seeking a well-fitted bra was to visit cramped, out-of-the-way lingerie shops whose saleswomen notoriously have a very liberal approach to personal space and privacy, giving new meaning to the word *intimates*. The experience is so outrageous, it was spoofed on the TV show *Broad City*, but people still go out of their way to receive this expert, albeit intense, shopping guidance. Now, women can get expert recommendations from the comfort of their homes, and it's yet another way that brands are doing the work for people. Focused recommendations create a service for consumers, which brings to light a repeating theme of how brands are successfully connecting with people today. Successful brands today embrace a reversal of the power dynamic: now more than ever, it's a buyer's market.

The notion that more choice is always preferable is a myth, because offering more choices so rarely benefits the consumer more than it does the brand. In so many cases, the distinctions among options are barely discernible to the consumer, more likely to create decision paralysis than a feeling of being deeply understood. Sure, people may like to pick out a color, but who enjoys their time in the toothpaste aisle? Or even worse, the distinctions in a category like baby formula, where parents are forced to choose between benefits like advanced immunity and easy digestion, both of which seem rather important? So many of these variations are created to give a brand "new news" (a redundancy that provides yearly fuel for the advertising industry), or to take up more space in a retail environment. But now brands can reach the exact people they're meant for, on those people's phones, their products available for immediate purchase. With that degree of precision in the brand-consumer relationship, the brand message and its offering need to be just as sharp. Instead of trying to hook as many people as possible by accounting for every possible need and preference, brands can connect with the right people from the start, over a shared idea that's bigger than any one product. This kind of day-one focus sets the stage for deliberate, purposeful growth over time, and lasting obsession.

Remember: Do the hard work of figuring out not just who you are, but who you're not. This enables you to be crystal clear about what you stand for. Not everyone is going to love you, but the ones who do will be obsessed.

6

REDEFINE EXPECTATIONS

I'M EMBARRASSED TO ADMIT THIS, BUT I REMEMBER RAIL-ing against the new colorful iMacs when I was in college. It was 1998, Apple had just released its candy-colored desktop computers, and as they started to show up in more and more dorm rooms, my initial reaction was that they looked ridiculous. Why would anyone want a brightly colored computer? It's silly, it stands out too much, it doesn't feel like a serious and powerful piece of technology. I shared these thoughts with my friend James, who said to me, "All umbrellas used to be black." It was such a simple statement, but it woke me up to a new way of thinking. Why does one need to default to the way things have always been done? More important, if there's an opportunity to transform something that was traditionally mundane into something more fun, more beautiful, and more interesting, we should embrace it. It would be a few more years until I switched to a Mac, but from then on, I had a new appreciation for brands that went against the grain. I began to seek out brands that shook me out of my comfort zone, making connections where I wasn't expecting to find them. I also now always choose the fun color version, and my umbrella is bright yellow.

BRAND CHANGES EVERYTHING

From launching with just one style, to rethinking naming conventions, to introducing emotional narratives into categories that were historically defined by the functional, the winning brands of today are writing a new playbook. In fact, the success of many of these brands comes from their boldness in completely reimagining how a business behaves. The word *disrupt* has become a startup cliché, but there's no denying the ways in which these brands are disrupting the status quo. Most of the clients we work with are looking to fundamentally change the perceptions and behaviors within a certain category, if not invent an entirely new one. People used to buy shampoo and conditioner in a drugstore based on a specific benefit; now they can have it custom made online with Prose. People used to overpay at a department store; now they can buy quality housewares with Snowe. And, of course, Uber and Lyft, while not Red Antler clients but a prime example, have so altered the way people order cars and pay at the end of a ride that I find myself, in the rare times that I take a yellow cab, about to leave without paying my driver (they begrudg-ingly assure me this happens *all the time*). These brands have suc-ceeded in changing our muscle memory, erasing the once automatic reflex to reach for our wallets at the end of a ride.

Technological innovation is a key ingredient of these widespread behavioral shifts, but brand is the engine that propels the change forward. Without a beloved brand that connects with people from the beginning and makes "new" feel not just palatable but desirable, it would be a lot harder to get large populations accepting a different way of doing something they've been doing their whole lives. In fact, there are some categories in which behaviors are so ingrained, it's hard to imagine how it could ever be different, until a brand comes along and changes everything. These businesses succeed by breaking all the rules, not haphazardly but purposefully, and—here's the key—always in favor of the customer. From their products to their stories, they demonstrate that there's actually a better way, and bring everyone along for the journey. This includes improvements like better customer service, greater transparency, and easier shop-ping experiences. But it also often means introducing a beloved brand into a category that previously wasn't brand driven at all. Perhaps the ultimate disruption is to prove that brand matters in places where it never seemed to matter before. Today, all the "unsexy," functional categories are up for grabs: contact lenses, renter's insurance, erectile dysfunction treatment. And no category has been turned more up-side down by brand than mattresses.

HOW CASPER CHANGED
THE RULES OF SLEEP

The mattress category has so fundamentally transformed in the past five years that it's hard to remember what it used to be like, and brand is at the epicenter of the shift. Today, you can open Facebook most days and find a heated debated in which everyone seems to have an opinion. "Friends, I'm thinking of buying a Casper—worth the hype?" "Leesa versus Tuft & Needle, what would people recommend?" From there, the comments flow, with the same amount of enthusiasm typically reserved for the World Cup or the latest Netflix show. Everyone is singing the praises of their pick, how easy it was or how reasonably priced or how quickly it arrived or, most important, how they've never slept better.

But there was a time, not so many nights ago, when no one talked about mattresses. It was something that every single person owned, and that very few thought about or cared about, at least from a brand perspective. In fact, unless you owned a Tempur-Pedic or had spent $10,000 on a Hästens, you may have been hard-pressed to even name your brand of mattress. (I think it's one of the *S* ones? Serta?) You most likely bought it in a showroom like Sleepy's, or perhaps a department store, trailed by an overeager salesperson. You possibly fell for one gimmick or another, after lying on a bunch of beds for a few minutes each, wasting a Saturday on this boring errand. And all of this felt not just totally normal, but essential—how could you ever buy a bed, one of the most expensive and important items in your home, without trying it? But once you bought it, the sheets went over it, and that was it, until you were in the market again a decade later.

When the Casper team arrived in our office, the business wasn't even called Casper yet. It was a team of five guys, a couple of whom my cofounder JB had met when he spoke at an accelerator program (programs to which aspiring startup founders apply, and in which they give away a portion of their business in exchange for capital, resources, and connections). At the time he met them, they had been working on their second business idea (Casper would be the third, and certainly the charm). The minute we sat down with them, we knew they were onto something. The idea: create a top-of-the-line mattress and sell it online direct to consumers at a fraction of the price, with none of the hassle. Philip Krim, the CEO, had prior experience selling mattresses online—he spoke passionately about the unnecessary middlemen and markups and inefficiency that only hurt customers in the end. Jeff Chapin, heading up industrial design, had an incredible pedigree and was making great progress working on a proprietary blend of foam that would not only be insanely comfortable and avoid the typical pitfalls of memory foam (which has too much "sink" and traps too much heat), but could also be compressed and shipped in a box. Which of course was key, because this was going to be an e-commerce business: with Gabe Flateman, leading technology, Neil Parikh in charge of operations, and Luke Sherwin heading up brand.

Of course, the question was, can this be done? Even with everything in place—great product, great team, excellent customer service, affordable price—how do you actually get someone to buy a mattress, from an unknown brand, without the opportunity to try it? People had all been trained that those three brightly lit, shoes-on minutes in the showroom were essential to guaranteeing your future sleepy happiness. If the showroom was some version of speed dating, what was this—a blind arranged marriage? Where everyone is given the same spouse?

That was another key piece of the equation. Casper, to start, was only going to sell one mattress. No soft versus medium versus firm versus some vague indicator like "700," or half the bed is a 700 and the other half is an 800. The Casper team was convinced that there's a bell curve of sleepers and that most people prefer the same medium firmness. I was skeptical at first. But then they made an excellent point—think about an amazing hotel bed. Everyone thinks it's comfortable. How is your bed at home any different? Not to mention they had a statistic that people who first try their mattresses in a showroom were actually less likely to be satisfied with their purchase. Casper's strategy of launching with one mattress and later expanding to a multi-mattress portfolio, along with sheets, pillows, and other products, is a perfect example of how focus can drive traction that paves the way for future growth.

Many investors were initially skeptical, but the Casper team knew that the time was right to upend this tired industry. The direct-to-consumer model was starting to show some serious traction, with companies like Warby Parker proving that goods like eyewear, once also thought to be strictly in-person purchases, could be sold online. Of course, Casper couldn't mimic Warby's in-home try-on model. What were they going to do—ship five mattresses and allow people to send back the ones they didn't like? And there had yet to be a hit in a category as utilitarian and unsexy as mattresses. So far it had mostly been accessories and fashion. But that was also the opportunity. The key to success was to build a beloved brand in a category that had largely been devoid of brand loyalty. The Casper team knew from the start that brand was a critical piece of the equation. An incredible brand, where no great brand had gone before: that's what would get people to trust this unknown company enough to take a chance on ordering a mattress online. Despite the Casper team's lacking a final name, even a final bed design, we were in.

THE LIMITATIONS OF TESTING

We knew that, in order to succeed, we had to completely break the rules of what had been done before. Because Casper was setting out to sell mattresses in a whole new way, we needed to build a brand that occupied a unique space, enough to get people's attention and convince them to think about their existing behavior differently. For an innovative business like Casper, the brand has two roles to play: shake people out of complacency (sure, you do it this way now, but why?), and then entice them with a new approach. Again, it's about striking a balance between the new/provocative and the familiar/comforting. It's the solution people never knew they were seeking.

As I've talked about, new is both an advantage and a liability, especially when people are used to things functioning in a certain way. All categories of goods or services, particularly those that have existed for a long time, have their own established set of tropes and traditions, and over time everyone comes to occupy roughly the same space as everyone else. There are subtle variations—that's how you can tell brands apart—but everyone follows the same set of rules, until a brand comes along, breaks those rules, becomes wildly successful, and puts new rules in place. You once walked down the cleaning products aisle and it was all bright bursts and sunny circles, until Method came along with its sleek, minimalist design and set a new standard. Apple is the prime example of a company that consistently breaks the rules of its category to its great advantage. From packaging to advertising, tech products are almost always sold by their features; the more bells and whistles, the better. Apple took the exact opposite approach with its understated elegance and focus on design, and was able to turn a piece of hardware into an object of desire, so much so that people care more about the brand than the products.

However, it's not as simple as deciding to break the rules. There's an incredible amount of risk involved, which is why so many brands, even new brands, stick to the lane that's already been established. It's even harder to break out of that lane when companies are overly reliant on consumer testing. Particularly with traditional companies, testing often happens every step of the way. For a new product to hit the shelves, you start by testing the concept. This is where you write up a description of the new product or service, sometimes with sample visuals attached, and gauge consumer interest—either in focus groups or an online survey or both. The idea is that you can determine whether you have a potentially successful idea on your hands before investing in the creation of the product. But for an idea that's truly groundbreaking, you run the risk of a false negative. After all, if people had seen a description of an unknown company that sells a mattress only on the internet, that ships in a box, without the benefit of a lovable brand, a beautiful website, incredible press coverage, and nearly instant word of mouth, would the data have predicted that they would fall in love?

The same risk applies when a brand launches a "minimum viable" or scrappy, 1.0 version to see if it sticks before investing in the full launch. While this may work in some categories, it's extremely difficult for a brand that's trying to break the rules with a consumer product. If Casper had launched with a bare-bones, barely branded website with stock photography that was trying to sell people an $850 mattress in a brown cardboard box, would it have taken off, making it incredibly difficult for the competition to catch its lead? Casper focused on brand from day one, which enabled it to break new ground.

But building a brand before launch requires leaps of faith at every step. In the old world, after a product passes the concept test, there's a whole series of additional research that occurs around product form, packaging, naming and logo design, and advertising campaigns. For many of the traditional companies whose products line the shelves and fill our homes, nothing gets released without extensively testing every creative decision. One might think this is a good thing because it puts the voice of the consumer first. But it actually puts the needs of the company first. It's used as a way to offset risk, to justify decisions, and to sell in choices internally (if it tested well, you're less likely to get fired when it bombs). This approach very rarely leads to better or more effective creative output.

Q: How can a business be confident in decisions without data to back it up?

Research can be extremely valuable in the early phases before product development, when you're trying to understand your target audience, go deeper on their needs, and identify problems to be solved. And testing is very effective in a live environment, e.g., run two Facebook ads and see which people click on, or A/B test two different versions of a landing page to see which converts better. There, you run no risk of false positives or false negatives, because you get the actual results. But it's impossible to create a brand that completely redefines its category if you're testing every decision before launch. Within a testing environment, consumers can very rarely identify what is actually going to motivate them. For example, shown a piece of packaging and asked to rank which product features are most important, they may say they're all important, which is how you end up cramming seventeen different points onto the front of the box. However, what you aren't able to predict is that in the store, they'll actually be drawn to the box that's simple and elegant and clean, the one that doesn't look like anything else. Or when given a description of an ad and asked to imagine it with a fun pop song, people may say it doesn't provide enough information, but if they were to see the actual ad on TV, they would have an emotional reaction and remember it days later.

It's even harder to test core elements like logos or names. Consumers are almost always initially drawn to what's most familiar, most literal, easiest to wrap their heads around. That's because they're being asked to make a rational evaluation rather than have an emotional reaction. They'll choose the name that most closely describes what the business does, even though, as I've discussed, a literal name ends up being quite limiting as a business expands beyond its initial offering. Or they'll select the logo that's an actual picture of whatever the business is selling, which misses the opportunity to tap into the subconscious power of design. It's not that consumers don't know what they want. It's just that it's extremely hard to articulate the desire for something completely new, especially in a testing environment, when you haven't ever been shown what that thing could be.

Of course there's power and reassurance in familiarity that should not be discounted. If consumers are used to associating certain things with a particular look and feel, from milk cartons to doctors' offices, that familiarity helps create a sense of trust and an ease of decision making. People have routines that they embrace, that provide a sense of stability and comfort to their lives. It's these ingrained rules that make it so noteworthy and exciting when a brand breaks out of the norm. But it doesn't work to be different just for different's sake. You can't haphazardly zig just because everyone else is zagging—if you could, it would be a lot easier to create a winning brand. You could just look at what everyone else is doing, and do the exact opposite, like George Costanza going against his instincts on *Seinfeld*. But it's not as simple as ordering chicken salad on rye, untoasted, instead of tuna on toast, and there's risk attached to veering left when everyone else is marching right. Typically, there are solid reasons that the competition is playing where they are: in many cases it's the result of research and refinement by the category leaders over many years. They know what works; in many cases, they've created what works.

You have to have a good reason for going against expectations, and you need to identify the places where you'll tap into what's familiar and comforting so that you have permission to break the rules elsewhere. In other words, you need a strategy, and it needs to be rooted in a consumer truth. When your goal is to transform a category, or create a new one, you have to start by asking: What can you stand for that no one else is owning, but that people actually care about? How can you carve out a unique space that's unlike anything that's been done before, but that will also resonate? When we initially set out to create Casper's brand strategy, we thought we would focus on the delight of the shopping experience. It felt like an obvious territory to own for an e-commerce mattress that ships in a box: here was the simplest, easiest, quickest way to "fall into bed." But as we started to explore this idea creatively, we realized we were missing something. If we wanted to build a beloved brand in a category that had to date been impersonal and utilitarian, we couldn't base the brand on an idea that was still pretty functional and based on convenience. Yes, convenience was one of Casper's benefits, but would you really care that the mattress arrived quickly if you didn't want it in the first place?

Casper saw an opportunity to stand for something bigger. From day one, its founders never set out to start a mattress company; they wanted to be a sleep company. So the natural question to ask was, Why does sleep matter? What role does sleep play in our lives? The competition certainly spent a lot of time talking about sleep. Take one quick stroll around a mattress showroom and you'll see all kinds of promises about how to get the best sleep ever known to man, not to mention a staggering amount of jargon that may or may not be rooted in real science. Trademarked terminology, clinically proven claims, various breakthroughs in the field of foam studies. It's enough to make you want to crawl under the covers. Caught up in the weeds of how to get a great night's sleep, no one was focusing on what a great night's sleep gets you. Sleep matters not for the six or eight or ten hours we spend in bed; after all, if all is going according to plan, you are not even conscious during that time. The reason sleep matters is because of how people feel when they wake up, and what that means for the rest of their day. The power of sleep is what it brings to people's waking lives. The brand strategy for Casper became the idea that better sleep leads to a more interesting life, and the team set out to build a sleep company that embraces the duality between going to bed and waking up.

From that point forward, every creative decision was made to celebrate the role of sleep in living your dream life. Through that lens, it was never just about the product—it was about how the product fit into a larger story about who people were, and who they wanted to be. This approach influenced every key decision as the brand was being created, finding every opportunity to thoughtfully and strategically go against the grain of what had been done before. Because the business started out as e-commerce, a tremendous amount of attention was paid to the website itself—finding many small moments to surprise people and defy their expectations of what a mattress company could be. Instead of using dry jargon to talk about firmness, there was an illustrated spectrum that ranged from a diamond to a gelatin mold, with Casper sitting perfectly in the middle.

Bios of the founding team could be toggled between "day" and "night," revealing who they were as people and as sleepers. Photography avoided all the classic clichés of people happily dreaming in bed, and instead showed people performing various quirky activities, from reading books about bird-watching to playing an under-the-covers game of mini golf.

There was also the mattress itself. Mattresses are rarely exposed, and they all mostly looked alike with white swirly patterns or generic off-white foam. Casper saw the opportunity to create an iconic design, even if it would spend most of its time covered by sheets and blankets. The Casper product team obsessed over how the mattress looked unmade, despite their knowing it would rarely appear that way. They created a two-toned design that set a new style for the category, and added a little branded tag that was closer to something you would see on a sweater or a pair of jeans than a mattress. That tag, though tiny and nearly always hidden, was an important creative decision for Casper, because it signaled that people were getting not just a mattress but a brand. In fact, you could make the case that the hidden nature of a mattress combined with the attention to detail actually deepened Casper's relationship with its customers: the design is there for you and you alone. Lastly, there was the box. Unlike the mattress, the box was an opportunity for prime visibility, and one of Casper's most powerful early marketing tools. The now iconic navy and white stripes announce themselves not only to the person receiving a Casper, but to every neighbor walking by—here is something different, here is something worth taking note of.

LIVING THE DREAM

Casper's commitment to defying expectations has continued well past launch. The choices that Casper makes are guided by improving the experience of its customers in some kind of fundamental way. When it breaks the rules, it's in favor of consumers. For example, shortly after launch, Casper had the opportunity to buy New York City subway media at a discounted price. At the time, the subway was a combination of one-off ads for plastic surgeons and dentists, and full-car takeovers by established brands like JetBlue. For those who haven't been to New York City, a full car takeover is when a brand buys every panel within one subway car to blanket the car and have more impact. Every direction you look, you see an ad from the same company, so you can't miss it. At a certain point, takeovers became best practice, and it's rare these days that you'll find yourself in a car with a multitude of individual ads. Standard format for these takeover ads is an assortment of (hopefully) clever headlines that each hit upon a different point of the business, with the logo repeated on every panel. When Casper decided to run ads on the subway, we had very little time to develop the creative idea and even less time to produce the campaign. But we knew we didn't want to look like everyone else.

At the time, Casper offered just one mattress, so we decided to run a campaign that would demonstrate that one mattress could suit nearly all sleepers. This could have been conveyed through headlines about how comfortable the mattress was, or how much people loved the mattress, or whatever else Casper wanted people to know in order to convince them that they could order a mattress off the internet and sleep very happily. But instead, Casper set out to create a campaign that would be "a gift" to New Yorkers. The idea was to offer an entertaining and interesting moment for people at the time in their day when they need it most: trapped in a crowded car hurtling through a dark tunnel, looking up to try to desperately avoid eye contact with fellow passengers. We created a campaign that was a celebration of all the different types of people who benefit from sleeping on a Casper.

We didn't focus on "side sleepers" or "back sleepers" or anything functionally connected to a mattress. Instead, we created a series of illustrations that brought to life a set of characters who celebrated the quirkiness and diversity of New Yorkers. We worked with artist Tomi Um, whose signature style became a core identifying element of the Casper brand. With Tomi, we built our colorful cast that included Lovers (two male Koala bears), Locals (a rat, a pigeon, and a squirrel enjoying a meal of pizza), Cool People (snowmen) and many, many more. And, of course, all were at home on a Casper, the "Perfect Mattress for Everyone." The idea behind the campaign was to give riders endless surprises to discover, and therefore make their ride go by a little faster. These weren't headlines you could read from across the car. You had to get up close, delight in the illustrations, discover the added humor that was buried in the details. Suddenly, being pressed against the wall wasn't such a bad thing, and people were often spotted forcing their way through a crowded car in order to read them all. We refreshed this campaign multiple times: first with a new set of characters, then moving into a narrative structure that showed what could happen when you "wake your best self" (scenes included a wolf finally blowing down the little pig's house, and a princess waking up and riding off on a moped without waiting for any kind of prince to show up and deliver that fabled kiss). After that, we created complex hidden-picture scenes that asked riders to participate in the puzzle by finding "more hours in the day" (hidden illustrations of clocks) or "more pie in the sky" (hidden pies, of course!).

The Casper campaigns became so beloved that many other brands tried to copy them by introducing their own cute illustrations, but what they missed was the attention to detail, the choices that were made for no other reason but to make people happy. Every illustration and corresponding caption were obsessed over, not for what they communicated about Casper, but for their humor, their surprise, their ability to brighten someone's commute. Of course, the idea of humor in advertising is nothing new. For practically a century, advertisers have cleverly woven entertaining stories to deliver a marketing message, like a spoonful of sugar to make the new extra-strength nighttime cough medicine go down. Sometimes, ads are barely related to the product they're selling, and it's a strategy of positivity by association—the commercial made you smile, so you'll remember the brand with good feelings too. This approach can backfire—I'm sure everyone has had the experience of absolutely loving a commercial and having no memory of what it was for, particularly around the Super Bowl. But the difference with the Casper campaign, whether consumers knew it or not, was that the motives behind the work were not just about the benefit to the brand. It was about using every opportunity to create experiences that exceeded expectations.

KEEPING IT FRESH

Q: How can a business continue to break the rules when it's no longer the challenger but the leader?

One of the greatest hurdles that a break-the-rules brand faces is how to stay rebellious as it grows. So many brands today launch in reaction to an industry—they see what's broken or outdated or inefficient and set out to fix it. And when a business is small, scrappy, and new, it's a lot easier to flout convention and reimagine how things should be done. Not only can you move more nimbly with fewer stakeholders weighing in on every decision, you also have less to lose, so it's not just easier to take risks, it's necessary. You have to make bold moves in order to get noticed, or you'll never get off the ground in the first place. As these startups begin to see success, they inevitably raise more money, sales targets become more aggressive, and expectations from investors soar. For example, a business may start out never offering discount codes, avoiding the transactional price wars of its category and instead opting for emotionally resonant, entertaining advertising. But over time, as a brand needs to continue growing, the increase in sales that comes from an aggressive well-placed offer becomes very tempting.

This is a constant struggle that many startups face—how to balance noteworthy, differentiated brand building with more-functional (and sometimes more immediately motivating) hard-hitting messaging. Luke Sherwin, one of Casper's founders, had a brilliant analogy that I think of often. He felt that Casper's "brand equity"—in other words, the love that people have for the brand because of all the ways in which it set out to delight them—could be thought of like marbles in a jar. Every time a business runs a transactional ad or any piece of communication that's focused directly on driving sales, it removes a marble from the jar. It's okay for you to remove the marbles—in fact, it's necessary to grow—but you need to also continue filling the jar, or eventually you'll have no more goodwill from which to borrow. So if you're going to run a bunch of "ten dollars off" ads, maybe it's also time to invest in an experimental pop-up.

It only becomes harder after new brands reach the initial set of consumers who fell in love with them for their rebellious spirit, and then find themselves needing to expand their audiences to those who may be more comfortable with conventional ways of shopping. The key is finding ways to grow on your own terms. This is the difference between brands that maintain their lovable spirit versus those who wake up one day to discover they've become their parents. One of the most important forks in the road is when digitally native brands move into physical retail. On the surface, it may seem surprising that direct-to-consumer brands are opening brick-and-mortar stores. Many of these brands—Everlane, for example—launched with a story about the efficiencies that come from selling online, purposefully positioning themselves against traditional, physical stores. They highlight the cost savings that result from eliminating middlemen and removing infrastructure, along with the convenience. And then they reach a point where they all open their own stores.

Q: Why are digitally native brands moving into physical
retail? Isn't it inherently contradictory to their whole
disruptive business model?

There is often a strong business case for moving into physical spaces. You are able to build awareness in a different way, and reach a whole new audience of people who may not be shopping as frequently online, or may not be open to shopping online for your category. Additionally, physical experiences provide incredible, unmatched brand-building opportunities if done correctly. No matter how beautifully designed a website may be, there is no substitute for entering a space and experiencing a brand with all your senses. But that only works if you continue to break the rules, instead of becoming the exact type of business you set out to unseat.

Launching physical spaces was particularly tricky for Casper, when so much of the early brand story was about the unpleasantness and, frankly, uselessness of the mattress showroom experience. We wrote copy that questioned why you would lie on a mattress for three minutes under harsh lights when you could try one for one hundred nights, to highlight Casper's one-hundred-night return policy. We celebrated that the original Casper mattress suited most sleepers, and that there was no reason to try fifteen different mattresses under the watchful eyes of a pushy salesperson when Casper had done the work for you. We created an entire brand experience that was meant to get people out of the showroom and into a bed that would make their lives better. But the time came in Casper's growth when it made sense to give people an opportunity to try the mattress in person. While massive numbers of people had proven that you could indeed sell a mattress online, sight unseen, there were still more people to convince, including those who loved the brand but wondered if the bed was all that. In the early days Casper had a couple of small spaces in New York and LA where people could come and experience the mattress, but these were more used as a sales tool for the customer experience team than treated as part of a larger retail strategy. Casper knew that when they inevitably made a serious move into retail, they would have to do so with a fresh approach that continued to defy expectations.

Casper began experimenting with some pop-ups, but its first noteworthy foray into the offline world wasn't a location, at least not in the stationary sense. A year after launch, Casper unveiled the napmobile—a roving vehicle with four individual sleep pods outfitted with Casper mattresses, sheets, and pillows. The napmobile took its Nap Tour across the US and Canada, stopping in cities to offer sleepy people everywhere the opportunity to book a nap online or just show up. In each pod was a timer with lights that represented the sun setting and rising, and there was even a phone that could be picked up to hear a bedtime story. When Casper launched its dog mattress, pups got their place on the napmobile too. Over ten thousand people took part in the Nap Tour, which gave them the chance not to just lie on a Casper but to actually sleep on one, in an environment that could not have been further from a traditional mattress store. As an added bonus for the brand, the napmobile was social media heaven, building surprise and love that reached far beyond those who got to experience it in person. When was the last time someone on your Instagram feed posted a picture of their trip to a mattress store? Or any traditional store, for that matter?

As the napmobile roamed the country, Casper was meticulously planning its approach to permanent retail, and opened its first stores in New York City in early 2018. Instead of putting rows of mattresses on display for all to see, Casper built semiprivate miniature homes within the store, each containing one of Casper's mattresses for people to experience at their leisure (at this point the offering had expanded to three models). Instead of signs that touted complex jargon or deals of the day, Casper took an approach that's closer to a science museum, educating people about the specialness of its products in ways that were straightforward, clever, and fun. The store feels less like a store than an experience, a place you might want to explore, not knowing what's around the corner. And the reinvention didn't stop there. A couple of months after launching its SoHo location, Casper launched the nearby Dreamery, a place where people can book naps. The Dreamery is near the Casper store, but it doesn't sell anything other than sleep itself. Your nap session comes with pajamas on loan, skincare samples, and an assortment of reading materials specifically chosen to "put you to sleep." Of course the hope must be that some of those who stop by the Dreamery for a nap will end up next door to buy their own Casper. But the intention of the Dreamery was more than a sales tool or a marketing gimmick. The Casper team is singularly devoted to its mission of providing better sleep for all. From the beginning, they wanted to improve how the whole world sleeps, rooted in the belief that great sleep is an essential ingredient to a great life.

Even if Casper faces future challenges, there's no denying it achieved something remarkable. I've had many people who don't even own the mattress tell me how much they love Casper. My former boss's five-year-old son begged her for a Casper for his bedroom. Casper has been able to create a more emotionally driven connection than was ever thought possible in its category, opening the door for what a brand can be. It fostered love by breaking the rules, creating a brand from day one that was totally different from what had come before. In order to drive obsession, differentiation is critical, in both product and brand. But differentiation also needs to be purposeful. Newness can't just be an attention-getting gimmick, because any initial excitement that you're lucky enough to build will flame out just as fast. For people to fall in love and stay in love, change needs to be in their favor. An innovative business needs to be designed to meet their needs in new ways, and the brand needs to be built to drive lasting and meaningful connection.

Remember: Figure out where and how you're going to break the rules, not just to make noise, but in service of your consumers. What can you do better for them that they've never experienced before?

7

EMBRACE TENSION

WHEN I WAS IN COLLEGE, MY FRIENDS AND I USED TO PLAY a game called the "two-adjective" game. You had to come up with the perfect two words to describe your "type," the perfect combination of attributes in a person that gets you every time. As nerdy as this sounds (and is), it was a fun, enlightening little exercise. Some people were terrible at the game, because they'd come up with stuff like *fun and easygoing. Sexy and hot. Tall and there.* These combinations missed the point, because they were too obvious and did nothing to paint a picture of an actual, specific type of person. Everyone wants to be with someone "fun"—choosing that word reveals nothing about you, nor the people you go for. The good answers, the ones that really nailed it, were the unexpected combinations. The goal was to come up with two traits that you wouldn't necessarily think of putting together but that, when paired, paint a really vivid picture. *Cocky and sheepish. Inexperienced and unamused. Rugged and goofy.* In the middle of all this, I never would have guessed that I could actually make a living with this kind of thinking, but now, years later, as I'm helping brands define their personalities, the same rules apply. The most interesting brands, the ones that people obsess over, have tension built into them. They play with the power of surprise.

THE MYTH OF CONSISTENCY

Historically, the very first lesson of Branding 101 was the importance of consistency. Pick a message and stick with it. Decide what you want to say, and then say it until you're blue in the face, until it's drilled into the hearts and minds of every person in the world and they can repeat it back with gusto. This lesson isn't completely off base, in that it is absolutely important to have a clear sense of purpose, and a single-minded idea of what you stand for. But the practice of consistency needs a twenty-first-century update. Clarity and focus, or internal consistency, are not the same as external consistency in messaging and marketing. Strict adherence to external consistency—how you show up to your audience—can be harmful to a brand's success when interpreted too literally. Too many brands think that they need to embrace consistency by looking the same and sounding the same everywhere they appear, like a politician (everyone's favorite type of person!) repeating talk points. That may have worked when all you had to worry about was a TV campaign and your packaging. But today, with so many channels of communication, each functioning differently in people's lives, it no longer makes sense, and it no longer feels real, to behave the same way everywhere.

Think of how an individual appears and behaves differently on LinkedIn versus Facebook, or even in their Instagram feed versus Instagram stories. They're still the same person. No one accuses them of being scattered or duplicitous. It's simply that each of these channels has its own set of cultural expectations, calling for different types of behavior, and people respond accordingly. The same is true for brands today. The most beloved brands understand how to adjust their message to the medium, from the beginning. That doesn't mean the brand stands for many different things. In fact, having a clear, single-minded strategy is what enables a brand to adapt its behavior depending on where it appears. The brand can take multiple paths, all in the direction of the same North Star. When a brand is clear about what it stands for, it then has the freedom to emphasize different facets of its purpose and personality depending on the time and the place, without diluting its identity. It can dress differently for the barbecue than it does for the cocktail party, standing out in every occasion for its impeccable style and not because it messed up the dress code.

Rather than staying in a tightly defined lane, successful brands today embrace contrast, mashing together ideas that may not seem obviously aligned but that come together into a unique and ownable identity. When a brand behaves in only one way, and it's the way

that everyone expects, there's no opportunity for the magic of surprise. The brands that challenge people's expectations are the ones
that stand out, creating richer and more-nuanced worlds that keep
offering something else to discover. When we are developing a new
brand, one of the steps of writing the strategy is to define the brand's
"personality," the way it behaves. And it's way too easy to fall back on
the same qualities every time—trustworthy, confident, intuitive.
Clients more often than not will ask us to include "trustworthy," and
we push back and say that trust is table stakes and does nothing to
carve out new territory. Try to name a brand that doesn't want to be
seen as trustworthy. That's not to say that it isn't important for
brands to be perceived as trustworthy. Rather, it's so important, so
obvious, that it's not worth mentioning. Instead, we try to find terms
that contrast with each other, creating combinations that have never
existed before, just like the two-adjective game I used to play with
my friends. This is how we ensure richness and nuance within the
brand. Casper, for example, is both pioneering and lovable. Its innovation is rooted in groundbreaking research, its team of engineers
is serious about changing the mattress industry, but the brand is also
cuddly and charming and witty. For every brand we create, we seek
those moments of tension that will lead to a memorable experience.
Brands that avoid tension in favor of consistency end up stuck in the
land of predictability. It's the unexpected layers that keep things interesting and keep people coming back for more, especially with so
many more ways to engage with a brand.

HOW SOULCYCLE USED CONTRASTING TRAITS TO BUILD ITS BRAND

Brands that embrace multiple facets of their personality, especially contradictory facets, end up creating experiences that feel much richer and more alive. You see this in a brand like SoulCycle, which played a significant role in transforming the workout space, inspiring an explosion of boutique fitness studios trying to capture the same magic. When SoulCycle opened its first studio in 2006 in New York City, the idea of indoor cycling was not new. Stationary bikes had been a dust-collecting fixture of dens across America for decades, and indoor cycling classes had been offered at gyms since the early '90s. But SoulCycle's founders, Julie Rice and Elizabeth Cutler, created an experience that was unlike what had come before. If you pick apart the attributes of the brand and examine them separately, it's hard to imagine how they could ever fit together. It's a symphony of antonyms.

First, you have luxury versus inclusivity. At thirty-six dollars for a single class, there's no question that SoulCycle is a luxury brand. Regular classes can quickly become way more expensive than a high-end gym membership. There's also an aura of scarcity, which often goes hand in hand with luxury: in certain markets, popular teachers' classes fill up almost the instant they open up online. It can be harder to get into a SoulCycle class than a hot new restaurant, which explains why some people pay for Soul Early, a feature that gives early booking access for an extra fifteen dollars a bike. The studios themselves contribute to the luxury feel: with bright white walls and fresh flowers, they look more like a premium boutique or spa than a workout space.

On the flip side, SoulCycle's brand is all about inclusivity. Wherever you are on your journey, you are welcomed. The front desk is always well staffed, with friendly faces greeting regulars by name and helping newcomers get set up. Philosophically, it's not a place that's only for the superfit or superthin; it "embraces every soul," as it says on its website. Teachers start each class welcoming new riders and reassuring them that it gets easier over time. In fact, the brand focuses much more on messages of personal transformation and human potential than on burning calories. Teachers routinely remind their classes that they're on a bike that goes nowhere, and therefore should have fun. Common logic might dictate that the two ideas of luxury and inclusivity cannot and should not live together. But the contrast clearly doesn't bother SoulCycle's avid riders. Consumers today want to feel they're part of something special, but they also want to feel completely welcomed there. The days of "I wouldn't want to belong to any club that would have me as a member" are over. Luxury has morphed into the value of an incredible experience, abandoning the old, cold ways of overt snobbery and exclusivity. People who can afford SoulCycle pay for it because what it offers them is worth the extra cost; it's a feeling and an experience they can't get elsewhere. And part of that feeling is feeling good about themselves.

Next, there's earnestness versus toughness. SoulCycle's brand is so earnest and open about its philosophy, it can almost feel dogmatic to an outsider. It describes itself as a "sanctuary," a "safe space to ride through whatever you're facing." There are mantras on the walls of its studios, with expressions like "we inhale intention and exhale expectation." The studios are lit by candles, and instructors often high-five everyone at the end of each class. Even the name itself implies a commitment to spirituality that isn't typically associated with hardcore workouts. But the brand also has a tough, unapologetic quality that keeps it from feeling too "kumbaya." Music blasts through the space. The best riders compete for the front-row bikes, with new riders encouraged to sit in the back. (The *New York Times* even wrote a story in 2015 about the status of the front row, and SoulCycle sells tank tops that read "Front row.") Though the official logo is a yellow bike wheel, much of its gear is emblazoned with a skull and crossbones, a secondary symbol that brings a rebellious, rock-star quality to the brand. Again, this combination of soft and hard, uplifting and competitive, is unique to SoulCycle and creates an experience that's hard to replicate elsewhere.

And it's not just surface level: the mantras and skulls are emblematic of a distinct approach to fitness that also represents a blending of genres. Instead of responding to specific instructions, riders move to the beat of the music, creating a rhythmic and immersive choreography that's more like dance than cycling. Unlike other cycling studios, there's no leaderboard indicating who's outperforming whom, but teachers constantly push riders to push themselves, challenge themselves, and avoid the trap of their comfort zone. They walk through the room, offering praise and encouragement. The overall effect is positive and uplifting, but within the context of an extremely arduous workout. Because, make no mistake, SoulCycle is very, very hard. Don't be lulled into a false sense of ease by the feel-good phrases on the walls. The workout's difficulty, and therefore efficacy, is what keeps SoulCycle's teachings from feeling heavy-handed or cheesy. People can embrace their spiritual side while sweating like crazy in one of the most challenging workouts they've ever done. Rather than feeling contradictory, it's right in line with a modern approach to self-fulfillment.

Instead of choosing between mind, body, and yes, soul, people want to care for all three, recognizing their interconnectedness in ways that borrow heavily from Eastern philosophy but are relatively new to Western culture. There was no personal journey component to the aerobics classes of the '80s. As people seek more than just sweat from their workouts, SoulCycle has answered that call, feeding a deeper need for a more holistic transformation that may include dropping a dress size but certainly doesn't end there. As brands reveal different sides of their personalities, they are effectively tapping into the different ways their audiences view themselves. It's giving people permission to exist in more than one way, to embrace their own contradictions. You can believe that "kindness is cool" (one of the rules of SoulCycle etiquette) while also being a highly competitive athlete. People don't see themselves as one-dimensional, and they don't want that from the brands they love.

However, while a brand can embrace tension when it comes to its tone, there is no room for inconsistency when it comes to the brand's values. You would appreciate a friend who is fun loving at a party and thoughtful during a serious conversation, but would feel less enamored of a friend who claims to be a hard-core environmentalist and then doesn't recycle. In the summer of 2019, SoulCycle and Equinox, the luxury fitness club brand that owns SoulCycle, faced controversy and protest when it emerged that their owner and chairman, billionaire Stephen Ross, was throwing a $100,000-per-head fundraiser for President Trump. For many consumers, any association with Trump flew in the face of what these brands were supposed to be about and who they were meant to be for. Both Equinox and Soul-Cycle claim to stand for inclusivity, diversity, and open-mindedness, which are not qualities typically associated with President Trump. Celebrities and activists called for boycotts, and SoulCycle saw a drop in its customers that summer. This is the catch of building a brand that's rooted in values: when it emerges that those values are not being upheld at every level, people feel betrayed. Of course, once you start pulling the thread on where the money comes from, it's extremely difficult for any brand to be blemish-free. But the SoulCycle incident proves once again that people are paying attention, and they want the assurance that the brands they choose are who they say they are. Playing with people's expectations is smart when it comes to brand personality, but not when it comes to a brand's core identity. Tension and flexibility are not the same as hypocrisy.

LETTING GO OF CONTROL

Q: I've always been told that consistency is the key to brand building. What changed?

The move toward brand flexibility, or "stretchiness," can be clearly traced to how the media landscape has evolved, and with it the role of marketing in people's lives. As you may know or have read about in a history textbook, it used to be that for the privilege of watching television, you also watched the commercials. They were an expected and tolerated interruption, and before DVRs, you simply couldn't do much about it. As much as ads felt less escapable back then, there was also a much clearer division between entertainment and advertising: with the exception of product placement, there was a "commercial break." Today, ad dollars still pay for our entertainment, just as much as they did before. You would not have the joy of seeing all your friends' baby photos and vacations and weird diets without advertising. But there's no longer a "commercial break." In fact, there's never a break. On social media, the brands are mixed in with everything else, whether it's through paid advertising, or, more miraculously, owned and sponsored content that people actually choose to follow and engage with. No one wants to feel they're being advertised to anymore, but on the flip side, people are voluntarily opting to hear more from the brands they love. The opportunity for brands is to create content that people actually want to see. With so many choices, people's attention has become a gift, and brands need to earn it by giving their followers something back. The brands that use social media most successfully are the ones who embrace its particular aesthetic and vernacular, rather than sticking to a strict definition of consistency. A highly polished, obviously curated approach may work well on a brand's website, but it's not what people seek on Instagram: not from their friends, not from influencers, and not from brands.

People engage with the brands they love on social media because it gives them a new, closer kind of access. Brands succeed now not by sticking out through glossy marketing, but by becoming part of the conversation. More and more, joining the conversation requires embracing imperfection, revealing a different and truer side of a brand's universe and its audience. Obviously, brands are selecting the images they post to their Instagram account with just as much consideration as the photography they choose for their websites. But for the first time in history, brands are able to feature "real people" and embrace a more approachable aesthetic effectively.

It wasn't always this way. When I worked in traditional advertising in the early 2000s, my team and I used to cynically groan in the back room of focus group sessions when people told us they wanted to see "more realistic" models who "looked like them." Sure, they sayyyyy that (we'd think), but time and again, the campaigns that worked best were the ones with the unattainably beautiful, impossibly skinny spokesmodels. We also had a similar skepticism when "user-generated content" (UGC) first became the rage in or around 2005. Brands saw UGC as a great opportunity not only to engage their consumers, but to generate a whole bunch of free content. *Time* magazine even named "You" as person of the year in 2006. However, most of the time, UGC looked terrible, and these poorly shot, poorly composed images of "real people" didn't work well on a brand's website. It simply looked messy and did nothing to drive desire or create connection. Things couldn't be more different now. Everyone's a photographer. Everyone's a model. Regular people can become overnight influencers, and celebrities post pictures of themselves popping pimples in the mirror. Most of the content you see daily is "user generated," and its aesthetic not only has improved with better cameras, but it's become the norm. The promise of UGC is finally coming to fruition. That doesn't mean that all brands can stop investing in photo shoots and rely solely on people's selfies. Again, it's about showing up the right way depending on context. The approach that works best on a website or a billboard is likely not the same as what works best on Instagram, and vice versa.

Brands that embrace actual user-generated content on social media, or at least adopt its look, more successfully embrace the medium than those who repeat the same approach regardless of where they're appearing. The social media content by brands that take too much of a polished, curated approach ends up looking too much like ads as people scroll their feeds, missing this opportunity to connect with their audiences on a more approachable and intimate level. Of course, embracing user-generated content as part of a brand's story does require relinquishing some control. As soon as you invite people to become part of the brand universe, you're letting go of any chance for perfect consistency. You can't control exactly what people are going to post, or the ways in which they'll make a brand their own. But the gain is far greater than the loss.

When brands are willing to let go of constant perfection, it opens up a world of opportunity to get closer to their audiences, by giving people greater access and ownership. An example of a business that has done well with this approach is the athletic-wear brand Outdoor Voices. Outdoor Voices was founded in 2013 by Tyler Haney. From the start, Haney set out to create a line of fitness apparel designed for everyday activities, not professional athletes. The brand's signature look is much gentler and more laid back than a lot of its hyper-technical, hyper-masculine competitors, but the clothing is still very much designed to perform. It quickly gained traction with its recognizable and highly Instagrammable color-blocked leggings and crop tops, attracting a buyer from J.Crew in the early days, which led to a collaboration that generated a ton of positive press. The Austin-based business grew from there, online as well as through its own physical retail locations.

The Outdoor Voices website features a nice range of body types, and the predominant impression is that of a moderately diverse set of very attractive people enjoying aspirational fitness activities like jogging through the desert. Where the brand really comes alive is through Instagram. Via its hashtag #doingthings (an abbreviation of the brand mantra, "Doing Things Is Better Than Not Doing Things"), Outdoor Voices gathers an impressively wide range of user-generated content. Throughout its feed, the brand celebrates real people of many different ages, sizes, and fitness levels, who are all out there having fun doing physical activities. While the brand still features its share of perfectly sculpted bodies, that content is balanced by imagery of regular people and their exercise routines, which elicits comments like "great choice for your model!" and "so nice to see models of all ages and body types!" and "killin' it!"

Much of this imagery is generated by Outdoor Voices' "brand ambassadors," who receive free clothing from the brand in exchange for posting. It's important to note that the brand has also received negative feedback for featuring plus-size models when it doesn't yet offer an extended range of sizes (as of 2019, it was "working on it"). But most of the commentary on the Outdoor Voices account is positive, with people applauding those featured in the posts, and the brand itself for featuring them. Outdoor Voices also generated a tremendous amount of buzz for running an ad that featured a model with visible cellulite, which stood out among the typical retouched imagery of the industry at large. Its fans and the press were thrilled to see this type of body-positive, authentic image coming from an athletic-wear brand, reflecting how real women look, even those who are in great shape.

In the past, if you were creating a fitness brand, the accepted approach would be to feature "aspirational" (read: unattainable) bodies, to offer people a dream of what could be achieved. It wouldn't have mattered that most people would never come close to glistening six-pack abs or perfectly smooth legs; the approach was to create an absolute, unwavering fantasy, with no room for reality to enter. But that's not what people are seeking from brands anymore. By unapologetically including cellulite in its ad, Outdoor Voices earned both trust and respect. It honored its audience by showcasing their reality instead of constructing an alternate photoshopped version.

At first glance, imperfections—wrinkles, scars, blemishes—in ads can be surprising because consumers have been trained over decades to expect extreme, almost cartoonish airbrushing. But brands are now challenging those expectations with great success. In fact, it's the glitches and flaws that make a brand more interesting. People no longer feel constrained in their own lives by strict definitions or boundaries, and the same is true for brands. Even the term *athleisure*, the category that gets assigned to brands like Outdoor Voices, represents a blurring of the lines. Haney, along with the founder of Lululemon, has publicly resisted the athleisure classification, assuming that it implies a sort of laziness or inauthenticity, a brand for people who buy the gear but never actually do the workout. But I love the idea, and I think it's a perfect example of how brands and their fans no longer need to stick to a script. You may wear your Lulu-lemons to hot yoga; I may wear mine to brunch. Workout gear doesn't need to just be for workouts, and workouts themselves don't need to be so serious, either, excluding all but the fittest. Everyone can go at their own pace, and have more fun.

CATCH THEM BY SURPRISE

Human beings are complex, multilayered bundles of contradictions, and so are the brands they fall in love with. Put another way, people are full of surprises, and brands need to be as well. A pitfall of consistency is predictability. When a brand tries too hard to stick to the script, it's impossible to keep things fresh and keep people entertained. While it's hard to remember a time before Uber became the evil empire everyone loves to hate, Uber did a phenomenal job in the early days of creating layers of surprise and stretch. The first version of the brand leaned hard into creating a high-end experience. The logo was a metallic silver *U* that almost looked like a comic book version of a luxury brand, and the only vehicles were premium town cars and SUVs (this was before its more economical offerings, UberX and UberPool). Even the name, Uber, speaks to excess and superiority. I'll never forget the first time I ordered an Uber in front of friends, and an Escalade pulled around the corner to pick me up from a Lower East Side bar. People could not believe their eyes, thinking I had a fancy driver at the ready. In fact, the brand's original tagline was "Everyone's Personal Driver." While the experience was incredible, the brand ran the risk even then of seeming out of touch, something created for investment bankers and Silicon Valley moguls. Except it had a sense of humor. On Halloween, the car icons in the app magically appeared as little broomsticks. On National Cat Day in 2013, it started its UberKittens program, delivering Ubers full of adoptable, adorable kittens to offices in major cities. How can you hate on a brand that brings you kittens to cuddle?

Of course, Uber did become very easy to hate through the years, with controversy after controversy involving everything from its founder, to its treatment of drivers, to its handling of surge pricing during public crises. Just like with SoulCycle, a brand's having questionable ethics is not the kind of tension that should be embraced, and no amount of cleverness is going to distract from bad press if a business is behaving poorly again and again. The public reaction to Uber's internal policies is yet another example of how a brand's purpose needs to start from within.

However, in the pre-scandal days, Uber's quirkiness vindicated the brand from seeming like it took itself too seriously. Here was this tech-driven, premium brand, but surprise, it's funny! Humor, particularly when it catches people off guard, is a powerful tool for humanizing brands and creating a sense of deeper connection. And a lighthearted touch is even more effective when addressing topics that are typically serious. When Red Antler was helping to create the website for Keeps, the men's hair loss treatment brand, we felt it was important to include a Hair Loss 101 section. This is a category rife with misinformation and false promises, and part of Keeps' mission was to set the record straight on what causes hair loss, and which treatments actually work. However, this section of the site ran the risk of being at best dry and, at worst, depressing. We knew that men were already anxious about losing their hair, and we didn't want to contribute to a negative state of mind. Toward the end of the page, after outlining the problem, causes, and treatment, we included an illustrated section of "things that do not cause hair loss," which includes hats ("your fedora is just ruining your life in other ways"), masturbation ("you do you"), and natural high testosterone ("sorry, we know it's nice to think you're just too manly for hair"). This section, buried pretty far down the page, acts as a reward for those who have taken the time to research, and creates a friendlier dynamic between the brand and its audience. It's a way of providing reassurance and comfort—yes, going bald is stressful, but we can also laugh about it (and we're here to help).

Recently, there have been a slew of brands that have addressed traditionally taboo topics with a prominent wink, delighting people with their candor while simultaneously breaking down stigmas and starting new conversations. Hims, a men's wellness brand that offers treatments for hair loss and erectile dysfunction, along with personal care products, made a big splash with its cheeky ad campaign for its generic version of Viagra. The campaign makes uses of cacti, bananas, and other oblong-shaped symbols to convey the difference between something that stands tall versus something, well, droopy. (You get the picture. And if you don't, that's the most I'm going to spell it out. This is a family-friendly book!) Hims' approach is a world away from the old erectile dysfunction TV ads depicting silver-haired gentlemen smiling knowingly at their wives across a candlelit dining room table. By employing wit, along with a sleek, modern aesthetic, Hims created a brand that's far more real and relatable, especially for its target audience of younger men.

Another brand that made use of a bold and stylish approach to break down taboos is Thinx. The brand, founded in 2013 after a successful Kickstarter campaign, is focused on its main product, "period-proof underwear." The underwear, which looks like regular underwear, is made from a highly absorbent material that can replace or supplement feminine hygiene products like tampons or pads (one pair is said to hold the same amount as two tampons). Because the underwear is washable and reusable, it's a more sustainable solution than single-use disposable products, and it addresses some people's health concerns about the safety of tampons, at least the nonorganic ones. Here was a category that had seen very little disruption in decades. The big brands (Tampax, Playtex, Kotex, etc.) could be counted on for steady but minor improvements in comfort and absorbency, but other than a growing but still very niche enthusiasm for the "menstrual cup," there hadn't been significant change since people stopped relying on belts.

Thinx offered a pretty remarkable innovation, something so new that it was almost difficult to believe. The brand had to overcome a lot of skepticism about how regular-looking underwear could absorb so much liquid, as well as the potential "ick" factor, justified or not. It needed to make a big impact, which meant getting people talking. In 2015, Thinx set out to run an advertising campaign on the New York City subway (part of the Metropolitan Transit Authority, commonly known as the MTA). The campaign was beautifully shot, with tasteful, minimalist design, and featured women wearing Thinx along with images of a grapefruit (clearly, fruit is a popular stand-in for genitalia), runny eggs, and the headline "Underwear for Women with Periods." On its own, the campaign took a bold and direct approach to a topic that was rarely addressed with any kind of candor. But what made it stand out even more was the controversy surrounding its run. According to Thinx, the MTA, through its partner Outfront Media, took issue with the subject matter of the campaign, and tried to limit the use of the word *period* as well as much of the imagery that was considered to be too suggestive. Before the campaign ran (or was even officially submitted for review by the MTA board), Thinx brought this battle to the public, speaking with multiple press outlets and posting a redacted email exchange with Outfront to the Thinx Facebook page. Thinx used this potential stumbling block as an opportunity to highlight the hypocrisy of public reaction to certain topics, noting that the MTA frequently ran ads for breast augmentation services, along with advertising that features scantily clad women. Thinx argued that the reaction to its campaign was solely driven by discomfort around periods, which of course are a natural part of life and an important health topic. Following social media outcry, the campaign ran without modification, and Thinx established itself as a voice that is committed to breaking down barriers. The following year, its subway campaign featured transgender model Sawyer DeVuyst in Thinx boy shorts, once again working to erase stigma and becoming the first menstrual product brand to feature a trans man. In 2019, Thinx ran its first national TV campaign, created by agency BBDO, which featured cisgender men and boys in commonly experienced period-related scenarios. A boy tells his father he thinks he got his period; a man finds a blood stain on his sheets. The ad ends with the line, "If we all had them, maybe we'd be more comfortable with them." As if to prove Thinx's point, certain networks were uncomfortable enough with the material that a different version of the ad had to be created, removing the scenes that showed a blood stain and a tampon string.

Thinx's commitment to its mission doesn't start and end with an ad campaign. The company has multiple giveback programs, including a partnership with youth-run nonprofit PERIOD to create free access to period products for US students, a puberty education program called EveryBody, and multiple efforts to expand access to period products and resources across the globe. Its site also includes an education section, "Periodical," that features articles about women's health and menstruation along with other topics ranging from pop culture to feminism. However, Thinx faced its own controversy in 2017, when its founder and CEO Miki Agrawal was accused of sexual harassment and inappropriate conduct. Agrawal stepped down, and a new CEO, Maria Molland Selby, was brought in to replace her. Through new training and new HR policies, Selby and the rest of Thinx's leadership worked to get the company's culture back on track. It was disheartening to hear these accusations against the founder of a company that had built its reputation on women's empowerment and was doing so much great work in terms of both communications and action. But Thinx's broader leadership acted swiftly and decisively. As of 2019, Selby was looking to expand the brand globally, and in September of that year, Kimberly-Clark invested $25 million into the company. While Thinx faces new competition and its ultimate success is yet to be determined, there's no question that the brand has already succeeded in starting a more real and honest conversation around periods. Its grapefruit has become an iconic and celebratory image, and its subway campaign is one of New York's most beloved. In fact, when Hims launched its cactus campaign with seemingly no resistance from the MTA, people once again lambasted them for the uphill battle that Thinx had faced for simply being real about menstruation.

LOGO SCHMOGO

From cacti to grapefruit, Hims and Thinx both made use of clever symbolism to deliver a refreshingly frank approach to previously taboo topics. In Thinx's case, its grapefruit is its Instagram icon, which raises another point about the myth of consistency. With so many places and ways for brands to appear, the era of logo dominance is over. Thinx's logo is a simple, elegant serif word mark, but the grapefruit is just as much a symbol of the brand. SoulCycle has its word mark and its yellow bike wheel, but is just as recognizable from its skull and crossbones. It's not that logos don't matter: they're a key expression of a brand's identity, and when done right, can communicate a good deal about a brand's reason for being. But they're one tool in the toolkit, and, particularly in the digital realm, it's increasingly rare for consumers to ever see a logo out of context. On Instagram, for example, a brand's icon always appears next to its name, which gives brands like Thinx the freedom to be a bit more playful and loose with their expression. When brands we work with become too obsessed with finding their "version of the Nike swoosh," we have to remind them that we're living in a different era than when Nike launched, and that it's actually more important these days to have rich and varied layers for storytelling versus one symbol that says it all. Brands also need to recognize that a logo alone does not create a

connection with consumers. When Mastercard made a big announce-
ment that it was dropping its name from its logo, and relying solely
on the two overlapping circles, my honest reaction was . . . who cares!
When do you see a logo without surrounding context, to even notice
the missing name? The move was made to signal that Mastercard is
more than just a "card" business, providing other tech solutions and
services to its customers. But that's a perception shift that needs to be
instigated through actions and experiences, not through a new logo
design. Logos matter as part of an overall system, and we spend many
weeks developing them to ensure they are expressing the right feelings
and ideas. But they're just a piece of the puzzle. When new potential
clients tell us they "already have a brand" because they have a name
and a logo, we have to educate them that a logo does not equal a
brand, and, in fact, overreliance on logos (and taglines) as the sole
brand expression is a sure path into a consistency rut. I see subway
ads that are just a brand's logo repeated in every panel, with headlines
next to it, and it's such a missed opportunity to create a moment of
connection with people. A logo repeated feels like advertising you
should ignore. A grapefruit gives people something to discover and
engage with—it starts a conversation.

REAL IS A LITTLE MESSY

From imagery to messaging to overall tonality, brands today build
love by recognizing that a perfectly polished approach no longer
speaks to people. People fall in love with brands that feel real and
relatable, more like a human than a corporation. Sometimes that even

means a brand can make mistakes and be forgiven, as long as those mistakes are dealt with swiftly and with genuine humility. A brand identity that stretches, that invites people in, is harder to control, but that's a good thing. Letting go of control is what allows consumers to become part of the story. Their content gets featured, they see themselves in the brand's narratives, and they feel more invested. Instead of a top-down approach, it's a conversation, and conversations are by their very nature unpredictable—at least the good ones are. If you know exactly what a brand is going to say next, why should you keep listening? Instead, brands create obsession by inviting their audience on a journey that has twists and turns, even cracks in the road, and it's a whole lot more exciting.

Remember: You should stand for one idea, but you can and must express that idea in many different ways. With all the places a brand needs to appear today, you have to bend and flex to keep things interesting.

8

MAKE IT PERSONAL

AS A FOUNDER OF A COMPANY, I HAVE STRUGGLED WITH my discomfort around self-promotion. I don't tweet, I don't blog regularly, I have a difficult time bringing my voice to the forefront of the conversation. Even in writing this book, it took me a while to get comfortable using *I* and *me*. Most of the time, I would prefer that the Red Antler brand speak for me, or let our work speak for itself. But I've had to learn over the years that there's no separating my identity, or my cofounders' identities, from the identity of the company we started. If we want to work with the best clients, and recruit the best talent, we have to put ourselves out there, even if it feels vulnerable or, actually, especially if it feels vulnerable. Potential employees will come for an interview after having listened to a podcast or read an article featuring one of us, and it gives them a deeper understanding of what we're all about. People want to know the people behind the company. It's advice I constantly give my clients and that I've had to give myself many times too. After all, if brand needs to start from within, then the place it begins is with the founders themselves.

HUMANS HUMANIZE

If you stop to think about it, it's funny that people talk about their "love" of certain brands. It's one thing to love a product, something you can touch and feel and use, but brands are an abstract concept. And yet, people do feel a connection to certain brands that goes beyond the transactional. It's almost as if they were talking about a person, not a company. This deeper relationship is what separates the runaway successes from the rest. People's obsession with these brands isn't just about how the products fit into their lives. Their love for these brands becomes part of their identity. And that only happens because these brands don't feel like faceless, soulless corporations, but rather like living, breathing things with personalities, opinions, and feelings. In short, they feel more human.

One of the key ways for brands to feel more human is . . . actual humans! Success is often driven by a founding team that forms an inherent part of the brand's story. Founders having a public persona is nothing new; look at companies like Ford and Disney, and of course more recently there's Phil Knight, Steve Jobs, Howard Schultz, Arianna Huffington. But in the internet age, the role that founders play in a brand's story has transformed. Rather than inhabiting larger-than-life, enigmatic personas, founders of many of today's beloved brands feel like people you could know. And in getting to know them, particularly with the unique level of access that social media provides, consumers are brought deeper into the world of the brand. It's a lot easier to root for a brand when you know who's behind it and feel a kinship with them. When founders speak publicly about why they started a company, it crystallizes the company's reason for being: there's an actual person or team who saw a need and set out to solve a problem. Even after these brands have raised multimillions of dollars, they maintain a feeling of approachability and intimacy through ongoing exposure to the people who started it all.

When we start working with a new company, we always have a conversation about the role of the founding team in the brand's narrative. Not every founding team wants to be a forward-facing part of the brand identity. Many don't want to "make it about them." That's when we explain that it's not about ego, it's about access. They don't need to put their face on the front of the box, but people want to know who's behind the things they buy. If consumers believe in the founders, it's an added factor in their excitement about supporting the company. It also reinforces people's own entrepreneurial dreams: I did it, and you can do it too.

Many times, a founding team's story is inextricable with the story of the brand. Their point of view is what drives the brand's point of view. This is particularly true when their reason for starting the company is inherently personal and tied to their own experiences. Think of a mom starting a baby-food company, or a doctor starting a new kind of healthcare company. If a founder has been in the shoes of their target audience and knows that audience's needs firsthand, or if a founder has direct experience working in the category they aim to disrupt, it lends both relatability and credibility. People can connect to the founders' reasons for starting the business, beyond just a desire to make money, which then helps consumers feel better about spending their money. In fact, we've struggled in the past when we're working with teams who don't in any way fit the profile of their target audience. That doesn't mean that every founder needs to directly reflect the people they aim to reach, but it's certainly powerful when consumers can relate to them and their mission. That's why so many of today's successful businesses are founded by teams with a deep and personal connection to what they're doing.

Q: What if I want to launch a brand that doesn't have a personal angle to it? What if I just want to brainstorm some business ideas?

One of the very first questions we ask potential clients is their reason for starting this particular business. And we always get more excited to work with entrepreneurs who have a personal answer to that question, versus "I wanted to leave my banking job, so I did a whiteboarding exercise to identify which consumer categories were most ripe for disruption." That's not to say that businesses born from brainstorms never succeed, but it's an advantage when not only is the idea smart, but the founding team is the right team for the idea. That connection could come from years spent working within a broken industry, or it could be a moment of inspiration, driven by a personal experience. Dave Gilboa, one of the founders of Warby Parker, frequently tells the story of how the inspiration for Warby came when he lost a pair of designer glasses and was horrified that he would have to pay $700 to replace them, far more than he paid for his new iPhone. That was the first moment that he stopped to wonder why glasses cost as much as they did, which set him on a journey to figure out how to change that industry. Founders who come to their business idea through personal experiences or revelations are inherently more passionate, and that passion is contagious—not just for the people working at the company, but for consumers.

IT STARTS WITH THEIR STORY

So many of our founders arrived at their business through a personal journey, such as Lauren Chan, founder of plus-size fashion brand Henning. Lauren heard us on a podcast and reached out to see if we would partner with her. We immediately fell in love with her and her story. She had moved to New York from Canada working as a plus-size model with Ford Models, and eventually became the fashion features editor at *Glamour*, overseeing the plus-size fashion beat. Through her experiences as a model, writer, editor, and, most important, consumer, she identified an unmet need in the plus-size space.

While the body positivity movement was starting to take hold, Lauren still couldn't find well-made, luxurious women's wear in her size. Even though two-thirds of American women are above a size 14, mainstream brands continued to either pay lip service to plus-size with very limited collections that quickly sold out, or they ignored plus-size altogether. Lauren found herself hacking together outfits through a combination of fast fashion and vintage men's blazers that she would have tailored. She believes that a lack of fashionable choices with high-quality materials holds plus-size women back, and told me, "I've worn everything from size 12 to size 20. Working in fashion, I was always the only plus-size person in the room, and I felt completely on the fringes. There's a total lack of representation as far as clothes and content. There's a lack of diversity on fashion teams, and it was inherent to me in the clothes I was able to wear. I was working with people wearing designer clothes every day— Céline, Dries Van Noten—and I wore Forever 21 because cheap fast fashion was all that fit me."

For Lauren, this issue extended beyond the struggle of assembling an outfit, because what women wear has so much influence on their lives. "First and foremost, I didn't feel as confident as I could, because I was insecure about wearing cheap fast fashion in a sea of designer dresses. And I was perceived as less capable, less put together, not on par with everyone else. *And,* I was a fashion journalist writing about designer clothes that I had never actually worn. This was a triple disadvantage for me. I kept thinking, one season someone will make high-quality clothes for women who are bigger, and no one did." In addition to her own experiences, through her years at *Glamour,* Lauren had heard from thousands of plus-size women who were incredibly eager to invest in great clothes but had nowhere to turn. Most of the choices available to them were cheaply made, smock-like dresses designed to hide their bodies, and relegated to the back of the store. They were left out of the fashion conversation, and the fun. So she quit her job to do it herself, creating the brand that was everything she had wished for: high quality, no compromises, engineered with plus-sized bodies in mind, and sewn in a factory in NYC alongside American designer brands.

Working closely with Lauren, we named her new brand Henning, and created an identity that was strong and fearless, while highlighting the thoughtfulness, craft, and polish that went into each piece. Our brand strategy was "wear your strength," celebrating the idea that with Henning, nothing can stop you. When our branding engagement ended, Lauren still had months until she would launch, as she worked through the design and manufacturing of her first collection. Typically, our advice is to keep a brand identity under wraps until the official launch: common practice dictates that you shouldn't "scoop yourself" until there's something people can actually buy. Most of our work with founders is oriented toward that launch moment, when the goal is to get as much press and traction as possible when the business goes live.

Lauren, however, was adamant about bringing her audience along on her journey. She released Henning to both social media and press before her site went live, and her instincts were spot-on. She recalls, "We launched social and email six months before product launch, for which people thought I was loco. But that was the most important six months of development on Henning. I was able to talk to my readers who had turned into followers who would turn into customers. The conversations we were able to have were envelope pushing: genuine, intellectual, informative, nitty-gritty. I was so thankful to connect to my audience on a personal level. And from a business perspective, I was able to ask if they wanted anti-wrinkle or stretch fabrics, what colors they liked."

Henning's Instagram account offered a behind-the-scenes look as Lauren prepared to launch her business, everything from sourcing fabrics to getting business cards printed. Lauren interspersed personal experiences from her time as a model, stories of successful women of all sizes, and reactions from real consumers that she gathered in focus groups and on social media. She brought to life the problem she was aiming to solve through quotes like "luxury is a world that has not been open to me" and "dressing cheaply hurts my ability to get ahead in business." And her community helped in other ways too: "Right before launch, we had an issue at our photo shoot where the armholes were too high in the blazers, and they felt too tight in the armpits. I didn't realize it until we had the blazer on five people. I was supposed to start production that week. I was in a full panic, but then I realized, why don't I ask everyone in our community to send me their armhole and bicep measurements? Hundreds of women did. Connecting with my community ahead of product launch, ahead of trying to make a sale—ahead of anything other than purely learning their problems and asking how we can fix them, that will have a forever lasting effect on the company. When we make mistakes, which we will make, we'll have empathy, we'll have people who want to help us fix it. They'll know they're talking to humans and not bots."

When she did launch in September 2019, it was to an engaged and invested group, who were eagerly awaiting her brand. They were obsessed before it had even arrived, and much of that engagement was driven by Lauren herself. She and I talked at length about the relationship between her as founder, and Henning the brand. She described how she views her role, saying, "I was hesitant about putting myself forward at first, because I didn't want this brand to read as a pet project by somebody who has a few followers on Instagram. I want it to be a billion-dollar business. But everything that performs best [on social media] is my personal story. And it's not just because I take cute selfies and respond to Instagram comments. This is a plus-size brand, run by a plus-size woman, who gets it. So many plus-size brands are not even run by women, let alone plus-size women, and you can tell by how the clothes are designed." I asked Lauren if she felt a founder needs to reflect their target audience, and she explained, "Look, on one hand, there's validity in people who are not plus-size women making plus-size clothes, because it validates the business part of what we're fighting for. It says, 'This is not just an emotional problem that we're solving.' This straight-sized man doing it says, 'This is valid from a numbers point of view.' It mansplains it! But there are easy tells when you don't have a founder who's connected in a personal way—what you post on social, what your product looks like." Lauren's connection with her audience enables her to be far more thoughtful about her offering. "Everything I engineered into the clothes are problems I knew how to solve because I've been there. My pants ripped up the back on the way to the biggest interview of my career, and I had to sit there with my butt out. Now Henning pants have a reinforced seam. I have sat in meetings with my chest peeking out, so I put a secret button between the buttons on our shirts. Those solutions probably cost a dollar."

Henning would not be Henning without Lauren, and she is wise enough to put herself forward and become an integral part of the brand's story. In fact, she considered the importance of her role in the narrative from the very beginning. She tells me, "When I left my job as a fashion editor, I thought I'd start a consultancy or make fit technology that would allow multiple brands to expand their sizes. But I'm not the right person for that." Her public-facing career at *Glamour* and as a model gave her access to opportunities—writing a monthly column, designing a collection with *Glamour* and Lane Bryant. She was a face that people could relate to, and she received countless reader letters, emails, and DMs with questions and stories. "The result of all that research was that I needed to start a brand of my own, where I was the voice. People related to me being a plus-size person on the inside of the fashion industry. There aren't a lot of us. I didn't want to waste that visibility by going behind the scenes to build a tech company. I'm lucky, and I owe it to our community to push that forward. I owe it to our community to be on the cover of *Fast Company*. My goal is to help people who have felt marginalized, to help them feel included."

Another founder whose personal experiences very much guided her journey is Abigail Stone. When we first met Abigail, founder of the direct-to-consumer candle company Otherland, she told us a story about her childhood. Growing up, her beloved grandmother always imparted her philosophy of "the extra verve of the added touch." The idea was to embrace the details that make a big difference. For example, Abigail shared, if you buy a bag of clementines from the grocery store, take a moment to put them in a beautiful bowl. It's a tiny act that positively affects your surroundings and your day.

Abigail adored her grandmother, and the initial working title of her business was Verve. She spoke to us about the power of lighting a scented candle, a small gesture that transforms your surroundings.

As she described the company's inspiration to me, "I became obsessed with candles in my twenties. I always wanted candles growing up; my babysitter had Yankee candles but my mom said absolutely no way. I finally got an apartment with friends, and I started buying candles. I would light one in the morning while meditating. Or after work or business school class, I would come home, watch *Game of Thrones*, and light a candle. A candle is a feel-good habit and ritual. It's tied into self-care, in our increasingly digital world: striking a match, becoming present in the room. But the candles with the fresh sophisticated scents and appealing design were way too expensive. If you bought one, you were afraid to light it." After our first meeting, Abigail brought us each a candle that was personalized with our names. As we were evaluating the potential for a new candle company, we talked about how deeply people care about their homes and the spaces they occupy, and that candles could be a relatively inexpensive way to create an entirely new ambience. We spoke to people who were obsessed with candles, buying new ones almost weekly. Different scents can transport you to different moods or mind-sets, which is ultimately how we landed on the name Otherland for the business.

Abigail is an integral part of Otherland's story. Her personal style, as well as her passion for art and design, very much influences the brand's aesthetic, particularly as she launches new collections and considers the themes that drive the scents and the artwork. She describes herself as a lifelong lover of art, who studied art history and then went to work at Ralph Lauren in art acquisition. Abigail's relationship to art is a key driver in how the Otherland brand comes to life. As she describes it, "Art is everything for us. We are visual first. The future of home fragrance has to be visual. To sell scent online, it has to be visually appealing to get you over the hump of not smelling it first. This applies to Instagram too. We use art to tell the story of each collection, each scent, and what it evokes. It's about memories and nostalgia. It's the product, the color, the label, the topper lid, the matchbox. And this continues into our content on Instagram stories. The scent is more than rose and red currant. It's the childhood memories of your mother making a warm-milk latte, it's washing out the sea salt from a beach day in the outdoor shower. We are selling experiential, consumable objets d'art."

Abigail's memories inspire each candle, which then get woven into the brand communications. For example, Stone Fruit, a scent in the summer 2019 collection, was inspired by beach vacations with her mother, who would stock up on Nantucket wild beach plum jam that the family would then save for February to remind them of summer. There was also Abigail's first job in New York as a ball girl at the US Open, which inspired the tennis-themed Match Point candle (smelling of cut grass, cucumber, and, naturally, tennis balls). She says, "We're in an era when nostalgia matters, because it's an antidote to digital fatigue. Scent is the strongest trigger of memory. I'll start with a mood board, where I do a brainstorm for memories, and put together what that might look like visually. Then I'll write a brief and meet with our perfumer. The magic happens when customers are inspired by our perspective to buy something that emotionally connects, and then they tell us their story."

In many ways, Abigail is the face of the Otherland brand. We made the choice to feature Abigail on the site's homepage, and she plays a prominent role within the brand's Instagram. While that may not seem unusual, most brands do not feature their founders on the homepage of the website. If the founder is shown at all, it's on an "About" page, and site photography typically features models who fit within the brand's lifestyle. But in the case of Otherland, Abigail embodies the lifestyle, wearing her signature bold earrings of which I've never seen the same pair twice (another commitment to the "extra verve of the added touch"). The business was born out of her own tastes and passions, and the brand's identity is intertwined with her own.

Of course, striking this balance isn't always easy, especially as founders need to navigate their own comfort with the spotlight. As Abigail puts it, "I had social media anxiety to get over, but Otherland is very much me and I am it. It would be impossible to separate us." And she rightly recognizes the value of her personal contribution to the Otherland world. She explains, "The idea is to connect with people, and people connect with people more than brands. We've got Otherland: the story, the collections, the inspiration behind them (my memories) but I also want to show the behind the scenes, the making of, what inspires me, the highs and lows of being a female founder." She shares her struggles too. This is where the difference between Otherland the brand and Abigail the founder comes into play. She differentiates it as such: "Otherland shows you the lifestyle and the product within it. There's a big focus on storytelling—it's developed, polished, and edited; it communicates clearly. On my personal Instagram, you just have to post. You have to show behind the scenes, and the authentic experience of being a founder. It's un-varnished, and it's not always a great story." But, of course, it's the best kind of story, because it's real, it's relatable, and it's human. Without

Abigail, Otherland would be beautiful on the surface, but lacking the soul underneath.

As is true with Lauren Chan, many successful founders arrive at their business idea when their own needs aren't met by existing brands. Instead of continuing to feel left out and marginalized, they build the business they want to see in the world. Tristan Walker is an amazing example of a founder who launched a successful brand inspired by his personal experience. As a black man, he grew frustrated by how most mainstream drugstore brands ignored the needs of people of color. In 2013, he created Walker & Company, with the goal of building "the Procter & Gamble for people of color." His first brand release was Bevel, a line of shaving products designed for black men, with a single-blade razor that works better than multiblade razors on coarse and curly hair, thereby preventing common problems like skin irritation and ingrown hairs.

In most drugstores across America, products that serve the specific needs of a black audience exist on the "black shelf," which typically occupies part of an aisle in the back of the store, and largely contains outdated brands that don't appeal to the modern consumer. With Bevel, Walker created a brand that addressed a specific issue and that people could be proud to support. He built a diverse team to grow the company, which first launched as direct-to-consumer before entering Target in 2015. The brand also enrolled barbershops across the country in a referral program, as well as taking over barbershops for events that engaged local communities in the brand story. It ultimately opened its own experiences in places like the Barclays Center in Brooklyn, and created a video series that celebrated the importance of the barbershop within black culture, featuring different iconic hairstyles.

Walker & Company's next launch was Form, a line of hair care for black women, which similarly set out to address specific needs that were largely ignored by the larger consumer products companies. In 2018, Procter & Gamble, the company that Walker set out to disrupt, purchased Walker & Company for an undisclosed sum that's estimated as somewhere between $20 million and $40 million, with Walker remaining as CEO. It's hard to imagine Bevel and Form seeing the same success without Walker as the driving force, and face, of the business. His personal connection to the problems he's solving brings an authenticity and relatability to his brands that's impossible to manufacture.

FOUNDERS AS A BRAND

With certain beloved brands, like Bevel, it's impossible to see them reaching the same heights without their founders. The success of beauty brand Glossier is inextricable from its founder Emily Weiss. In college, Weiss interned at MTV, making a few appearances on the reality TV show *The Hills*. Her growing interest in fashion led her to an internship at *Teen Vogue*, followed by roles at *W* magazine and *Vogue* after graduation. In 2010, seeing a gap in beauty coverage within the fashion market, she started *Into the Gloss*, a blog where she interviewed models, beauty and makeup moguls, celebrities, and influencers on their daily beauty routines and favorite products. The site became wildly popular, starting an online dialogue with a community of more than two million (and counting) readers, with far more active commenting and conversation than the major women's magazines. While Weiss had had a lot of exposure to beauty tips from working fashion shoots, she didn't feel a connection to traditional cosmetics companies, who talked "at" their consumers and didn't reflect real women or their lives. Through the conversations taking place on *Into the Gloss*, she learned that many women felt the same way.

Launching her own line of products was a natural progression for Weiss. It started with her approach of creating a "two-way conversation" with her *Into the Gloss* audience, in stark contrast to how she saw the traditional beauty industry operating at a remove from its customers. Based on feedback from her community about the types of products they were seeking, and what was missing from the current landscape, Weiss launched Glossier in 2014 with four products. In service of Glossier's philosophy of "skin first, makeup second," its first set of products were its Milky Jelly cleanser, Balm Dotcom lip balm, a priming moisturizer, and a misting spray. To create the Milky Jelly cleanser, Weiss polled her *Into the Gloss* readers, asking: What would your dream cleanser look like? Smell like? Feel like? Do for you? Not do for you? Who would play this cleanser in a movie? She received more than 380 responses, and in doing so learned that women were frustrated at having to use both a makeup remover and a face wash, so she created a cleanser that does both.

Glossier is credited with championing the "no-makeup makeup" look, and it certainly doesn't hurt that Weiss is a natural beauty herself. The aesthetic it highlights is "glowy, dewy skin," with products that "bring out your best." More important, the brand says that "makeup should be the fun part, not the fix." In many ways, the brand is the no-beauty-industry beauty brand—launching independently, direct to consumer, with a bold, minimalist identity that stands in stark contrast to the heavy golds and bronzes and dark purples of the category. Glossier's brand is bright and poppy, consisting mostly of black, white, and pink, which not only positions it as a modern alternative to the stodgy department store makeup counter brands, but also shows up beautifully on Instagram. Scrolling through people's "shelfies," you can't miss the strong black Glossier logo. The fresh, minimalist look of its products mirrors that of its models, and both look great in a photo feed.

Glossier also seems to take itself less seriously than the rest of the industry, embracing fun and positivity. Its products ship in pink Bubble Wrap packaging, with a set of playful stickers for customization. The brand aims to "democratize beauty" and celebrate the individual. When it launched its first line of body products, Body Hero, the accompanying campaign featured nude women of all shapes and sizes, including plus-sized model Paloma Elsesser and Olympic medalist basketball player Swin Cash. By 2018, the company had surpassed $100 million in annual revenue, and its most popular product, Boy Brow, apparently sells at a rate of one every thirty-two seconds.

Committed to Weiss's two-way conversation, the brand stays in close contact with its customers, particularly through a constant influx of direct messages and posts on Instagram. For every new product launch, Glossier starts by listening to its consumers, testing and getting input to ensure the business continues to respond to real needs. The brand credits much of its growth to its engaged audience, who post selfies of themselves using Glossier products, and interact with the brand on Instagram, as well as through its city-specific Slack channels and at pop-up events.

From the early days of *Into the Gloss*, Weiss set the tone for a beauty brand that's on the level of the people it's trying to reach. While many brands claim they want the identity of your "in-the-know best friend," Glossier actually pulls it off. It's a brand that people feel they have real access to, including to Weiss herself. Instead of feeling corporate and stodgy like much of the beauty industry, Glossier feels like a community, with real people driving product development, and real people featured in its Instagram feed. The company describes itself as a "people-powered beauty ecosystem," and Weiss has described her customers as her "cocreators." She's a role model, but one who shows up in the comments section alongside her customers.

Traditionally, companies would only speak to people through the brand voice. You don't hear from the actual people who work at Estée Lauder; you see an ad for one of its products. You don't know who's responsible for the product development, or the ad, or the overall growth of the business. It just exists, born parentless from anonymous corporate-land and appearing before you in a magazine. Maybe an executive will make a statement in times of news or scandal, but that communication feels totally separate from the world of consumer brands. Now, founders are part of the narrative. Of course, Glossier the brand has a voice that's separate from Weiss, and Weiss has her own identity that's separate from Glossier. Each time that

Glossier communicates, it's not literally Weiss speaking. But we still get to hear from her directly, quite often. When it's time for Glossier the company to speak, whether in an article or on social media, it's not some corporate spokesperson or faceless customer service representative. She is out there, sharing her point of view.

Regardless of how much deliberate messaging strategy is going on behind the scenes with these founders, it feels like you have casual and open access to them. They're showing up on panels and podcasts where they're promoting a vision, not plugging a product. They have personal Instagram accounts where they get giddily excited about business milestones, and people root for them like they are friends who just had a great win at work. It requires a level of comfort with blurring the line between founder identity and brand identity, which is not for every entrepreneur. But when done right, it strengthens people's connection to a brand when they're a fan of the people who started it.

FAMOUS AS FOUNDERS

Weiss has become a celebrity through her journey as Glossier's founder, but there's another trend now of celebrities becoming founders. Of course, brands have historically aligned themselves with celebrities through endorsement deals and ad campaigns, hiring famous people to be the "face of the brand." What's happening now is stars who are either investing in new companies or starting their own, taking on the role of founder and business leader rather than spokesperson. Whether it's Jessica Alba with the Honest Company, Reese Witherspoon with her Southern-inspired lifestyle brand Draper James, Khloé Kardashian with Good American, or Kristen Bell and Dax Shepard with baby product brand Hello Bello, celebrities are taking an active role in launching and growing startups. And they connect the story of the brand with stories from their personal life; for example, Bell and Shepard emphasize their role as parents, not actors, in Hello Bello's messaging. Even George Clooney, when talking about the origin of Casamigos, paints a picture of a group of friends just casually hangin' out in Mexico, dreaming up the perfect tequila and deciding to create it for their own drinking pleasure (which ended up selling for a cool $1 billion to Diageo, no big deal). Who hasn't sat around drinking and brainstorming business ideas with their friends? We could all be George!

When Michelle Pfeiffer approached us for help launching her new fragrance brand, we were immediately drawn in by her mission. When Michelle first became a mother, she started paying more attention to the ingredient labels on all the products she was using, everything from food to beauty. Many moms go through this journey; in fact, from all of our work on clean beauty brands, we've learned that becoming a parent is a key moment when people start looking for safer products. Michelle began switching over all of her products, but the one area in which she couldn't find a better alternative was fragrance. As she dug in, she discovered that fragrance brands aren't even required to share their ingredients, because they've been able to hide under the cloak of "trade secrets." In fact, the term *fragrance* is a catchall that could include just about anything.

Michelle stopped wearing fragrance altogether, and then began a years-long journey to see whether it were possible to create a luxury fragrance using only ingredients that are deemed safe by the Environmental Working Group (EWG), a nonprofit dedicated to protecting human health and the environment. When Michelle came to us, she was finalizing the formulations of her first five fragrances. The strictness of her standards was unprecedented in the industry, and developing the scents had been a massive but exciting challenge for her and the fragrance house. Each of the scents was born from her own memories of people, places, and experiences. We came on board to help Michelle and her cofounder Melina Polly create a brand that spoke to luxury and quality, but also safety and sustainability. That brand became Henry Rose.

Henry Rose is the first fine fragrance brand with 100 percent ingredient transparency. It's both EWG Verified and Cradle to Cradle Certified, which led to very specific material and recyclability requirements when it came to the bottle and packaging. The brand is a study in contradictions. Responsible and sexy normally don't go hand in hand, but we embraced the tension between transparency and mystery, safety and sensuality. Michelle wanted to turn the fragrance industry on its head, and she pushed us to bring in imagery that plays with expectations around gender, beauty, and luxury.

While most fragrance brands will describe how something smells, often using misleading terms that don't line up to the actual ingredients (e.g., "musk" or "vanilla"), we instead created descriptions and imagery that evoke a feeling, playing with the idea of scent memories. The resulting brand identity is both intimate and cinematic, a modern brand that taps into nostalgia. More important, Henry Rose could not be further from a celebrity fragrance brand. From Elizabeth Taylor to Britney Spears, there's a long history of celebrities lending their names to a fragrance in order to create instant brand appeal. But in the case of Henry Rose, Michelle is the founder, actively running the business with Melina. This is no licensing deal: it was born out of her passion and of her years of hard work. On the homepage of the site, her name appears at the very bottom, but we don't lead with her image.

This is the opposite of our approach with Abigail and Otherland, because we didn't want Michelle's considerable fame to distract from the Henry Rose story. Instead, she wrote a letter on the "About" page that explains her mission in creating the brand. Her role in the story is her personal connection to the problem she set out to solve. She isn't there to lend her famous face to sell more bottles. You could see an ad for Henry Rose on Facebook and not even know its connection to Michelle Pfeiffer, and her name is not on the bottle. Of course Michelle is beloved and admired as a film star, but she's relatable as a mother and a committed founder who is looking to transform an industry.

Q: Brands have been relying on celebrities to sell products forever. How is this any different?

Consumers want to feel a genuine connection to the founders of the brands they support, and that doesn't come from a famous person blindly lending their name to any old product through a licensing deal. Celebrity involvement obviously gives new businesses an incredible advantage: an instant platform for press, a built-in audience of fans. But people are becoming less impressed by just seeing someone's face in an ad. With so much more access to information, consumers are savvier than ever before, and far more resistant to anything that feels like a marketing gimmick. In the absence of an authentic relationship to the business, a celebrity endorsement carries less weight. It's a meaningless added layer, versus an inherent part of the brand story. This is true for influencer involvement as well. While many brands have seen success tapping into influencers, consumers are getting much smarter about sniffing out, and rejecting, the influencers who will post an #ad for anything. There needs to be a plausible relationship between the influencer and the brand, a reason this particular person has credibility in this particular category. Otherwise, it's just a shameless plug, and people see through it.

TEAM MATTERS

If brand needs to be baked in from day one, then nothing matters more than the team behind the brand, and that starts with the founders. When a new business launches, founders set the tone, both internally and externally. There's an assumption among startup founders that coming up with an idea automatically makes you the right person to start the business. But what would it look like if more would-be entrepreneurs asked themselves if they're actually the best person for the job? The vast majority of startups that receive funding are run by white men, and that's not what the consumer landscape looks like. That doesn't mean that every founding team needs to exactly mirror their target audience. It's great that people want to apply their passion and expertise to creating businesses that serve wide audiences, especially audiences who are different from them. I certainly don't want all the white male founders only making stuff for people who look like them (that is *not* the lesson here)!

But let's just say you're a guy who has an idea for a company that largely makes products for women. It might make sense—crazy idea—to bring on a woman as a cofounder, to make sure you're walking the walk and not just talking the talk. We worked with an all-male founding team who was considering using a feminist icon as part of their brand identity, and we advised them against doing so. Their intentions were good, but it felt false to borrow feminist imagery for a brand that's being run solely by men. Founders who have less of a connection to their target audience are also more likely to question their instincts and decisions. We will hear concerns like "we don't think this idea will appeal to people outside of New York and San Francisco" (always voiced by people who live in New York or San Francisco), or that a proposed design "doesn't feel 'feminine' enough" (always voiced by men). Again, it's great that teams are thinking about the people they ultimately need to reach, but it can become dangerous when that concern takes the form of assumptions that are often unproven and unfounded.

People are paying more attention than ever before to who's behind the things they buy. They want to support not corporations, but teams they believe in, which is why new companies are launching in which the founding team is an inherent part of the brand story. Before assembling that team, it's worth considering who can credibly be the face of the business, with press and, even more important, with consumers. Who's going to be out there talking about it, who's going to be responding to people's comments on Instagram, who's going to help people feel heard and understood. And it's not just about public perception. It's about ensuring that you're building a brand rooted in insight and empathy from day one, that you have a deep understanding of the problem you're solving for the people you're hoping to reach.

Founders also drive internal culture, which directly influences the outward success of a brand. If employees don't have a deep understanding of a brand's purpose, if they aren't living and breathing it every day, then maintaining the magic as a business scales can be very difficult. Founding teams need to work to ensure their brand is infused within their company, treating their employees as their most important customers. This can happen through formal exercises like developing a clear mission statement and set of values, and it's also the little details that infuse the brand into a company's culture. Warby Parker gives every new employee a notebook and the brand's official style guide, along with a bag of Martin's pretzels, the snack that the mom of Neil Blumenthal, one of the founders, would bring in for the team in the early days of starting the business. This small touch connects new hires to the first days of the company and invites them to join the journey.

When the Skimm moved into a larger office, founders Carly Zakin and Danielle Weisberg empowered their team to design the space themselves. They worked with a paint company to mix a custom color that matches the brand's exact shade of blue, and named every conference room after a *Law & Order* character, in honor of

Zakin and Weisberg's early days of writing the newsletter from their couch with *Law & Order* on in the background. Founders are also finding substantive ways to demonstrate their brand values internally, such as Boxed CEO Chieh Huang, who pays for his employees' weddings and kids' college tuition. These companies understand that brand is not an external layer; it must be embedded at every level, baked into the very DNA of the business itself. It starts with the founding team, and then needs to be instilled in every subsequent hire. That's how you build a brand that people love through and through, from day one and well into the future.

> *Remember:* If brand needs to start from within, it begins with the founding team. Even if you don't exactly mirror your target audience, you need to embody the values and the spirit of the brand you seek to create.

CONCLUSION

*Q: So that's it then? Can I just build a brand based
on these principles, and ride the bullet train to success?*

The most common misconception that I encounter is the idea that
a "brand" is something you create, and then you move on. Brand
is a living, breathing thing. It's the culture you continue to build
among your internal team as you scale, it's all the ways you appear
and behave, and it's how you evolve your story and offering as the
world changes around you. Even after you've done the hard work of
figuring out what you stand for and why it matters, there's an incredible amount of art and skill involved in translating those ideas into
your consumer-facing expression, and keeping that expression fresh.
I've stated repeatedly that your brand is more than your logo, but the

external expressions of your brand are critical in that they form the impressions that help people understand what you're all about, and that ultimately drive obsession. In other words, the details matter. Thoughtful design and clear, compelling messaging are what get consumers to pay attention and invite you in, as well what keeps them engaged over time.

I didn't spend a whole lot of time talking about design in this book, but that's not because design isn't important; it's because this book is about the principles that need to drive design in order for it to be effective. The most salient and unspoken power of design is not that it looks cool or sleek or sexy; it's that it conveys an idea and is often able to do so more effectively than stating the idea out loud. Think about trust—the second someone says, "Trust me," you want to do the opposite. But a brand that consistently invests in great design and execution gives an impression of trustworthiness and legitimacy, which is particularly important when launching something new into the world. If you're asking people to whip out their credit card for a business they've never heard of, you sure don't want them wondering if it's a "real business." No matter how exciting your business idea is, building a connection through brand only takes on increased importance when you're launching something new. As much as people claim they want excitement and freshness, it's hard to change ingrained behaviors. With the exception of a small slice of the population who are true early adopters, most people are pretty comfortable doing things the way they always have. Contrast that with the fact that most startups set out to transform a category or even create a new one, and the challenge is obvious. It's not easy to get people to buy something online that they've always touched and experienced in a store, even if it's more convenient. It's not easy to get people to think about their health differently, or to stop buying the brand they grew up with. In order to create a lasting shift and ultimately take over as the new category leader, you need a brand that connects with people at every level: strategically, aesthetically, and emotionally.

However, once you've succeeded in building that connection, you can't sit still. Once your new and better way becomes the norm, how will you defy expectations once again? If you don't continue to nurture your relationship with your consumers, you'll quickly become the old guard that someone else sets out to disrupt.

Consumers fall in love with brands because of the ongoing, positive role these brands play in their lives. That's why it's so important to get it right from the beginning, and to continue to breathe life into your brand as it grows. You need a clear sense of purpose that will guide all decisions and behavior, and you have to find new and surprising ways to express that purpose. You need to create valuable, memorable, delightful experiences at every step. Ultimately, obsession comes when you build a brand that's 100 percent in service of its audience. Brands that succeed today are the ones that wake up every day and behave in a way that recognizes and honors the shift in power dynamic between consumers and businesses. With more choice than ever before, and traditional gatekeepers removed from the equation, consumers are running the show from literally the palm of their hand. Some like to call these new beloved brands "millennial brands," but millennials are simply the generation who came of age at a time when consumers were able to demand far more from the businesses with whom they choose to engage.

The values associated with these startups are not unique to millennials; they are values that nearly everyone shares. Transparency, authenticity, better customer service, corporate responsibility. Not to mention simplicity, ease, and—never to be underestimated—fun! The appeal of these brands transcends age or geography. They tap into the mind-set of a more empowered consumer, one who sees every choice as a statement about themselves, and who will go out of their way to support the brands they believe in. And it's not just consumers who are obsessed with the brands they love. Founders need to be obsessed too. They need to be obsessed with finding new ways to deliver value and joy. They need to be single-mindedly focused, from day one, on building a brand that's on the side of the people it aims to reach. And they need to realize that that work is never done. For those who say they can't afford to think about their brand yet, my question is, Can you afford to wait?

ACKNOWLEDGMENTS

Thank you to Allison Hunter at Janklow & Nesbit, for not only reaching out and setting this whole thing in motion, but for being an incredible agent, advocate, and friend through this entire process.

Immensely grateful to the entire Portfolio team, for your brilliance, passion, and support—"obsessed" with all of you! Kaushik Viswanath, thank you for believing in me from the start, and for all of your insights and guidance that helped the manuscript take shape. Thank you, Adrian Zackheim, for your vision and spirited conversation. Thank you for all your amazing work to Nina Rodríguez-Marty, Jen Heuer, Marisol Salaman, Nicole Mcardle, Meighan Cavanaugh, Jennifer Tait, and Angelina Krahn. And a massive thank you to Trish Daly for coming aboard with total enthusiasm, offering your invaluable feedback, and shepherding the book over the finish line.

I am deeply grateful to Ashley Hong and Vanessa Ting, my researchers extraordinaire who are proof that the future looks very bright, and that we just need to step aside and let Gen Z take over already. Thank you as well to Lauren Marino, for your help at the start of this journey.

Thank you to Pamela Peterson and Barbara Henricks at Cave Henricks Communications, for your belief in the book and your tireless work supporting it.

Thank you to all of my clients at Red Antler, for putting your trust in me and inviting us to be part of your stories. I am so fortunate to work with the most inspiring entrepreneurs and marketers in the world! To name just a few (because otherwise this section would be as long as the book): Philip Krim, Neil Parikh, Gabe Flateman, Luke Sherwin, Jeff Chapin, Joey Zwillinger, and Tim Brown, Julie Channing, Tina Sharkey, Geoff Bartakovics, John McDonald, Steve Gutentag, Demetri Karagas, Irving Fain, Katie Seawell, Adam Braun, Melina Polly, Michelle Pfeiffer, Charlotte Cho, David Cho, Pat Dossett, Blake Mycoskie, Stuart Landesberg, Jordan Savage, Will Matthews, David Lortscher, Fabian Seelbach, Neka Pasquale, Paul Coletta, Bill Smith, Susan Feldman, Ali Pincus, Mike Russell, Tom Currier, Gaetano Crupi, Chieh Huang, Justin McLeod, Katie Hunt, Holly Thaggard, Amanda Baldwin, Michael Petry, Laurie Spiro, Sophie Kahn, Bouchra Ezzahraoui, Farryn Weiner, Ania Goldberg, Jon Stein, Jason Hirschhorn, Jesse Kirshbaum, Ray Landgraf, Brandon Mills, Alex Weindling, Ryan Bonifacino, Stephen Kuhl, Kabeer Chopra, Nick Stern, Chris Jackson, Justin Urich, Adam Goldstein,

Brett Adcock, Louisa Schneider, Matt Miller, Charlie Hughes, Josh Udashkin, Simon Huck, Nick Brown, Susan Sarich, Ben Hindman, Charles Gorra, Chris Lotz, Dan Di Spaltro, Jay Bregman, Connie McDonald, Pam Weekes, Caroline Hadfield, Holly Whitaker, Matt Gamache-Asselin, Diksha Idnani, Scott Johnsen, David Utley, Busy Burr, Bassima Mroue, Matt Daimler, Susan Daimler, Palo Hawken, and Andrew Gordon. Special thanks to each of you who generously gave your time to be interviewed for the book: Oliver Sweatman and Emily Doyle from Ursa Major, Andres Modak from Snowe (thank you Rachel Cohen, too!), Arnaud Plas and Paul Michaux from Prose, Lauren Chan from Henning, and Abigail Stone from Otherland. I also want to thank Miko Branch of Miss Jessie's, who is not a client but an amazing founder, and who was so kind to share her experiences with me.

Thank you to the staff of Dumbo House for providing the perfect environment in which to write and a whole bunch of cold brews.

Thank you to all the writers I admire, particularly those to whom I reached out for advice along the way, notably Jonathan Fields, Linda Rottenberg, and Scott Belsky. Scott, you get a special shout-out for being the reason we started Red Antler in the first place, and an amazing supporter at every step.

And speaking of Red Antler, there would be no book without this incredible team. All of you are why I even have a thing to say on the topic of brand building, and I learn from you every day. A special thank you to Rafaela Sanchez and Nikole Ortiz for creating, and then fiercely guarding, the space for me to write. Thank you to Jonah Fay-Hurvitz for teaching me so much and making it so fun. Thank you to Blake Lyon for working tirelessly to bring us the absolute best client partners. Thank you to Beau Brown and Haynes David, my favorite Southern gents, for helping our business grow and thrive. Thank you to Hannah Lindsey and Julia Page for continuously showing me how it's done. Thank you to Ada Mayer and Jenna Navitsky, for your constantly inspiring creativity, and your cover advice! Thank you to Kelsey Rohwer, for shining light on the work we do, as well as being instrumental to the success of the book—truly would be lost without you. A huge thanks to Marni Kleinfeld-Hayes, for reading an early draft and offering your always spot-on feedback. Thank you to honorary Antlerist Mark Silver of Factory PR, for being the coolest and sharing some of that cool with me. Thank you to Red Antler's #1 supporter and dear friend Corbin Day, for the countless ways in which you've helped us succeed. And last but absolutely not least, a supersize, flashing-in-lights thank you to my cofounders JB Osborne and Simon Endres—you are truly the best partners and friends I could ever have asked for. JB, from the Friday afternoon I showed up on your doorstep at Spring Street, leading up to our conspiratorial chat at Aroma, I'm eternally grateful that I followed my mom's advice and "hitched my wagon to your star."

I can't imagine achieving anything, let alone writing a book, without the love of my friends and family. Thank you to: Ben Christen, Ali Winter, and Rachel Feierman—"we made it," and I surely could not without you. Emily Wallach, for your unabashed enthusiasm from the second I told you I was working on this—you gracht me. Emily Griffin, for your wisdom and guidance throughout this process. Jill Kauffman, for teaching me everything I know about strategy, mentorship, and shoes. My hilarious and disturbing gang, The Seat Steelers: Tiffany Graeff a.k.a. Agitator, Corrie Schankler a.k.a. Snacks, and Nadine Nicosia a.k.a. Volumizer—boom! Rachel Maimin, Alissa Bersin, Alex Marson, John Roberts, and Elyse Steinberg, for all of your support, this past year and always. Nano Wheedan for being you, and for always being there for me. Thank you to Sprouty, my tough little gal. Thank you to Dallas Desjardins. Immeasurable thank yous to my entire creative and funny and brilliant family: Grandma and Papa; Ellen and Kiki; Laura, Joel, Sierra, and Isaac; Charlie, Lizzy, and Henry; the D.C. Heyward crew; Tony and Myrna; Aaron; Jocelyn, Nikko, and Hero; and especially Sarah, David, Mom, and Dad, for your unconditional love and encouragement.

Thank you to Jake for being a constant source of lightness and joy. And above all else, thank you, Jess, for everything. You're my best friend, my partner in all endeavors, and the love of my life.

INDEX

accountability, 68
affordability and price, 30–31,
    53–54
Agrawal, Miki, 168
Airbnb, 16–23, 62
    Experiences, 21, 22
airbrushing, 162
Alba, 192
Allbirds, 1, 35–43, 68, 104
Amazon, 31–33, 110, 112, 119
American Apparel, 55
Android, 49
Apple, 36, 41, 49–50, 125–26,
    132
    iMacs, 125
Applegate Farms, 82
athleisure, use of term, 162–63
athletic apparel, 160–63
authenticity, 29, 77
Aviator Nation, 72
Away, 103–8, 112–13

Barber, Dan, 81
Barclays Center, 186
BBDO, 167
Beautycounter, 60–61
beauty industry, 60–68,
    187–91
Bed Bath & Beyond, 106,
    108
Bell, Kristen, 192
Bevel, 186, 187
Blecharczyk, Nathan, 17
Blumenthal, Neil, 197–98
BMW, 51
Bombas, 88–90
Booker, Christopher, 10
Books Are Magic, 32
Bowery, 44–45
Boxed, 33–34, 198
brainstorming, 176
Branch, Miko, 115–17
Branch, Titi, 115–17

brands, xiv–xv, 2–3, 5, 9, 199
    brand equity, 143
    brand idea, 8, 15
    brand name, 40–41, 45, 134–35
    brand strategy, 7–8, 15
    defining, xvi–xvii
    differentiation and, 4
    of existing businesses, 5, 62–63
    external expressions of, 200
    founders as, 187–91; *see also* founders
    importance of, 26–27
    as living, breathing thing, 199–201
    logos, *see* logos
    "millennial," 201–2
    personality of, 152, 153
    stretchiness of, 157, 171
Breast Cancer Awareness Month, 85
Broad City, 123
Brown, Tim, 35–36, 39–41
business models, 22

Care/of, 121–22
Casamigos, 192
Cash, Swin, 189
Casper, 30, 128–31, 133, 136–47,
        152
    Dreamery, 146
    napmobile, 145–46
causes, 85–90
celebrities, 192–95
Chan, Lauren, 177–82, 186
Chanel, 51–52
Chapin, Jeff, 129
charitable organizations, 85
Cheesecake Factory, 115
Chesky, Brian, 16–18
Chez Away, 105
Cho, Charlotte, 67
choices and options, 102–3, 109, 111, 112,
        118, 122–24, 201
    customization, 117, 119–22
    false distinctions, 102, 118
    see also focus
Chopt, 79
Clooney, George, 192

Coca-Cola, 29
    Diet Coke, 76
Cohen, Rachel, 107–10
Colugo, 1, 30
connection and community, 75–98
    causes and, 85–90
    chain businesses and, 80
    language and, 94–97
    Sweetgreen and, 78–84
conscious capitalism, 87
consistency, 150–52, 157, 163, 169
consumer insight, 7, 14
consumer needs, 10–15, 24
consumer research, 9–10, 13, 134–35
control, letting go of, 157–60, 171
convenience, 31, 33
core drivers, 11
corporate social responsibility (CSR), 90
Costco, 33
CPG (consumer packaged goods)
        brands, 25
Cradle to Cradle Certified, 193
Craigslist, 16–18
Credo, 60
CrossFit, 78
customization, 117, 119–22
Cutler, Elizabeth, 153
Cuyana, 59–60

Dalton Maag, 21
dating apps, 4, 68–72
death, fear of, 1–24
Del Ray, Lana, 82
design, 2–3, 135, 200
    user experience (UX), 3–5
DeVuyst, Sawyer, 167
Diageo, 192
Diet Coke, 76
direct-to-consumer model, 99–103,
        130–31
    and moving into physical spaces, 143–46
Disney, 174
disruption, 126, 127, 201
Doyle, Emily, 63–67
Draper James, 192

Drybar, 113–15
DVRs, 101, 158

early adopters, 9, 200
Earthbound Farms, 45
Elsesser, Paloma, 189
emotions, 13, 25–47, 93
  Allbirds and, 36–40
  Boxed and, 33–34
  functional benefits and, 28–30, 38, 40,
    47, 53
Environmental Working Group (EWG), 61,
  193
Equinox, 156–57
Everlane, 52–59, 143
EveryBody, 168
expectations, redefining, 125–47, 152, 201
  Apple and, 125–26, 132
  Casper and, 128–31, 33, 136–47
  growing companies and, 142–43
  reasons for, 136

Facebook, 69, 77–78, 92, 100, 128, 134,
  151
Fain, Irving, 44
familiarity, 135, 136
  see also expectations, redefining
fashion industry, 51–60, 177–82
Fast Company, 182
fear of death, 1–24
fitness apparel, 160–63
Flateman, Gabe, 129
focus, 99–124, 150
  Away and, 103–8, 112–13
  Care/of and, 121–22
  customization and, 117, 119–22
  Drybar and, 113–15
  Miss Jessie's and, 115–17
  Prose and, 118–21
  Snowe and, 107–11
  ThirdLove and, 122–23
Follain, 60
FoodCorps, 84, 86
Ford, Henry, 9, 11
Ford Models, 177

Ford Motor Company, 174
Form, 187
founders, 173–98, 202
  as brands, 187–91
  celebrities as, 192–95
  Chan, Lauren, 177–82, 186
  reasons for starting the business, 175–76
  Stone, Abigail, 182–86, 194
  teams as, 175, 176, 195–98
  Walker, Tristan, 186–87
  Weiss, Emily, 187–92
fragrance industry, 192–94
functional benefits, 41
  convenience, 31, 33
  emotional connection and, 28–30, 38,
    40, 47, 53
  price, 30–31, 53–54
  sustainability, 37–38, 68, 81, 120

Gallardo, Karla, 59
Gebbia, Joe, 16–18
Gilboa, Dave, 176–77
Gillette, 29–30
Girl Talk, 82
Glamour, 177, 178, 182
Glossier, 187–92
GNC, 122
Goby, 1, 30
Goldberg, Randy, 88
Goldman Sachs, 122
Good American, 192
Google, 3–4
Gucci, 52
Gutentag, Steve, 13

hair care, 113–21, 186–87
Haney, Tyler, 160, 162
health and wellness, 121–22
Healthy Child Healthy World, 61
Heath, David, 88
Hello Bello, 192
Henning, 177–82
Henry Rose, 193–94
Here, 105
Hims, 165, 168–69

Hinge, 68–72
HomeAway, 22
Honest Company, 192
Honest Tea, 82
Huffington, Arianna, 174
Huang, Chieh, 198
humanization, 174
humor, 92, 140, 141, 164–65

Ikea, 107, 109
inclusivity, 120, 123, 157
    luxury versus, 153–54
Indiegogo, 88
Instagram, xix–xx, 56, 66, 78, 94, 98, 100,
        151, 158–61, 169, 180, 181, 184,
        189, 190, 197
Into the Gloss, 187–88, 190

Jammet, Nicolas, 79
J.Crew, 161
Jobs, Steve, 9, 174
John, Daymond, 88

Karagas, Demetri, 13
Kardashian, Khloé, 192
Keeps, 13–15, 30, 164–65
Kickstarter, 35, 36, 166
Kimberly-Clark, 168
Knight, Phil, 174
Kondo, Marie, 59
Korey, Steph, 103–4
Kotex, 166
Krim, Philip, 129

LaCroix, 75–76
Lamar, Kendrick, 82
Lane Bryant, 182
language, 94–97
LinkedIn, 151
logos, xiv, 4, 22, 32, 35, 38, 46, 52, 57,
        169–70, 200
    Airbnb, 20–22
    Allbirds, 41
    Bombas, 89
    Boxed, 34

Hinged, 69–71
    testing of, 134–35
    Toms, 87
London, Theophilus, 82
L'Oréal, 118
loyalty, 106
loyalty programs, 83
Lululemon, 162–63
luxury, 51, 52, 54, 57, 61, 65, 107, 120–21
    inclusivity versus, 153–54
Lyft, 3, 41, 126

Mailchimp, 40–41
Marlboro, 29
Mastercard, 170
Match, 68, 69
Match Group, 69, 71
mattresses, 128–29, 138, 144
    Casper, xv, 30, 128–31, 133, 136–47, 152
McDonald's, 80
McLeod, Justin, 70
menstruation, 166–69
Method, 132
Metropolitan Transit Authority (MTA),
        166–69
Michaux, Paul, 118–21
Microsoft, 41
millennials, 201–2
Miss Jessie's, 115–17
Modak, Andrés, 107–11
Morris, Toby, 41
music, 82–83, 91–93
Mycoskie, Blake, 86

needs, consumer, 10–15, 24
Neman, Jonathan, 79
newness, as advantage and liability, 8–9, 131
New York subway ads, 139–41, 166–70
New York Times, 155
niche brands, 100
Nike, 36, 55, 169

Obama, Barack, 43
"obsessed," use of word, xix–xx
OkCupid, 68, 69

options, *see* choices and options
Organicgirl, 45
Otherland, 182–86, 194
Outdoor Voices, 160–62
Outfront Media, 167
overstock.com, 40–41

Pampers, 51
Parikh, Neil, 129
passion, 91, 97
Patagonia, 97
PayPal, 22
Peretti, Jonah, 55
PERIOD, 168
personal, making it, *see* founders
Pfeiffer, Michelle, 192–94
Plas, Arnaud, 118, 120
Playtex, 166
Polly, Melina, 193, 194
predictability, 163
price, 30–31, 53–54
problem solving, 5–10, 24, 27, 28, 32, 38, 46
    Airbnb and, 19–22
    Venmo and, 23
Procter & Gamble, 186, 187
Prose, 118–21, 126
purpose, sense of, 94

Ralph Lauren, 183
realness, 170–71
Red Antler, xv, 1, 2, 4, 7, 25, 27, 30, 103, 126, 164, 173
Reimagining School Cafeterias, 84
Renfrew, Gregg, 61
research and testing, 9–10, 13, 134–35
Rice, Julie, 153
Ross, Stephen, 157
Row, the, 52
Row 7, 81
Ru, Nathaniel, 79
Rubio, Jen, 103–4
rules, breaking, *see* expectations, redefining

Schultz, Howard, 174
Selby, Maria Molland, 168

sense of self, 49–73
    beauty industry and, 60–68
    dating apps and, 68–72
    fashion industry and, 51–60
Seven Basic Plots, The (Booker), 10
Shah, Shilpa, 59
Shark Tank, 88
Shepard, Dax, 192
Sherwin, Luke, 129, 142–43
simplicity, 102–3
Skimm, the, 95–97, 198
Slack, 79
slang, 95
Snowe, 30, 107–11
social media, 77–78, 158, 160, 175, 179, 180
    Facebook, 69, 77–78, 92, 100, 128, 134, 151
    Instagram, xix–xx, 56, 66, 78, 94, 98, 100, 151, 158–61, 169, 180, 181, 184, 189, 190, 197
Soko Glam, 67
Solazyme, 35
SoulCycle, 153–57, 164, 169
Spotify, 91–93
Starbucks, 80
Stone, Abigail, 182–86, 194
Straight-at-Home, 113
Strokes, 82
Subaru, 72
Subway, 80
subway ads, 139–41, 166–70
surprise, 152, 163
sustainability, 37–38, 68, 81, 120
Sweatman, Oliver, 63–67
Sweetgreen, 78–84, 86
    Sweetgreen in Schools, 84
    Sweetlife, 82–83
symbolism, 169

Tampax, 166
Target, 116, 186
Tata Harper, 60
teams, founding, 175, 176, 195–98
tension, embracing, 149–71
    SoulCycle and, 153–57

Terminal A, 105
television:
    commercials on, 158
    TiVo and, 101
testing and research, 9–10, 13, 134–35
Then I Met You, 67, 68
Thinx, 166–69
ThirdLove, 122–23
Thirty Madison, 13
Time, 159
Tinder, 4, 68–69, 71, 72
TiVo, 101
Toms Shoes, 37, 86–88
Trump, Donald, 157
trustworthiness, 152, 200
Tumi, 104–5
"two-adjective" game, 149–50, 152

Uber, 3, 126, 163–64
Um, Tomi, 140
Ursa Major, 62–68
user experience design (UX), 3–5
user-generated content (UGC), 159–60

values, 52, 68, 81, 83, 84, 86, 90, 97, 98,
    156–57, 197, 202

Venmo, 22–23
Viagra, 165
Vitamin Shoppe, 122
Vrbo, 22

Walker, Tristan, 186–87
Walker & Company, 186–87
Walmart, 116
Warby Parker, 36, 53, 87–88, 103, 130,
    176–77, 197–98
Webb, Alli, 113–15
Weisberg, Danielle, 95, 97, 198
Weiss, Emily, 187–92
Whole30, 76
"why test," 11–12, 28
    for Airbnb, 18–19
Wieden+Kennedy, 71
Wirecutter, 99
Witherspoon, Reese, 192

Y Combinator, 17
Yeah Yeah Yeahs, 82

Zakin, Carly, 95, 97, 198
Zimmerman, Edith, 79
Zwillinger, Joey, 35–36, 40, 41